Orby Shipley, Antonio de Guevara

The mysteries of Mount Calvary

Orby Shipley, Antonio de Guevara

The mysteries of Mount Calvary

ISBN/EAN: 9783743305700

Manufactured in Europe, USA, Canada, Australia, Japa

Cover: Foto ©ninafisch / pixelio.de

Manufactured and distributed by brebook publishing software (www.brebook.com)

Orby Shipley, Antonio de Guevara

The mysteries of Mount Calvary

ASCETIC LIBRARY

Vol. I.

The Mysteries of Mount Calvary

RIVINGTONS

London .... *Waterloo Place*
Cambridge .... *Trinity Street*
Oxford .... *High Street*

The Mysteries of Mount Calvary

TRANSLATED FROM THE LATIN OF

ANTONIO DE GUEVARA

EDITED BY THE

REV. ORBY SHIPLEY, M.A.

RIVINGTONS

London, Oxford, and Cambridge

1869

Preface.

ANTONIO DE GUEVARA, whose "Mysteries of Mount Calvary," after long neglect, is now re-introduced to devout English readers, was born about the year 1470, and died in 1544. He was a Franciscan of considerable learning and ability, and of exemplary piety. He became Bishop of Cadiz, and afterwards of Mondonedo. Charles the Fifth entertained a high opinion of his worth and talents, and made Guevara his Chronicler and Court Preacher.

He wrote excellent Spanish, and was Author of several works, amongst others of the following:—

A Life of Marcus Aurelius Antoninus, as an example to Princes, published at Seville in 1534, 4to; Madrid, 1658, 4to; translated into French by N. de Herberay, Paris, 1550, 8vo; and Antw., 1592; an Italian version, 1562, 4to; the same in Latin, with notes, by Johan. Wanckelium, Torg., 1601, fol.; and again, 1611. In

English it was published under the title of "Dial of Princes," translated by Thomas North, with a fourth book called the "Favoured Courtier," London, 1568, 1619, fol.; also, translated by Sir Francis Bryant, entitled, "A Looking Glass for the Court:" composed in the Castilian tongue; with sundry apt notes in the margent by T. Tymme, minister, London, 1575, 8vo; Lond. 1619, fol.

Another work of Guevara was his "Oratorio de Religiosos y Exercitatio de Virtuosos," Valladolid, 1542; this was published in Latin at Cologne in 1614, as "Oratorium Religiosorum," in 12mo. There are also French editions: "L'Oratoire des Religieux, et l'Exercise des Vertueux," traduit de l'Espagnol en Français par Paul du Mont, Douysien, Douai, Jean Rogard, 1576, 8vo; the same, 1583, and 1599: another translation into French, by N. Dany, Abbé de S. Grespin le Grand de Soyssons, Paris, Guillaume Chaudière, 1572, 8vo; id. 1582.

The "Familiar Epistles," or "Golden Letters," of Guevara, contain an account of the Spanish insurrection of 1522; and from their partisan character have gained for the author the title of *Mendacissimus* from Heumann. Of these "Epistles" the following editions have appeared: "Epistolas Familiares," Ital. Ven. 1545—59, 3 vols., 8vo; Venice, 1565, 4to: under the title "Epîtres Dorées et Discours Salutaires,'

Lyons, 1588, 8vo: in English, entitled, "The Familiar Epistles of Sir Antony of Guevara, Preacher, Chronicler, and Counsellour to the Emperor Charles the Fifth: wherein are contained very notable Letters, excellent Discourses, curious Sayings, and most natural Reasons: wherein are contained, Expositions of certaine Figures, Authorities of Holy Scripture, very good to be preached, and better to be followed; Declarations of Antient Stampes of writing upon Stones, Epitaphas of Sepulchres, Lawes and Customs of Gentils; Doctrines, Examples and Counsels for Princes, for Noblemen, for Lawyers and Churchmen; very profitable to be followed, and pleasant to be reade:" translated out of the Spanish tung by Edward Hellows, Groome of the Leashe. London, 1574, 4to.

"A Dispraise of the Life of a Courtier, and a Commendation of the Life of a Labouring Man:" translated by Sir Francis Briant, Lond. 1548, 8vo. His "Encomium on Rustic Life," translated into English by H. Vaughan, London, 1651, 8vo. "Il Dispreggio della Corte, e Lode della Villa, trad. Cosimo Baroncelli," Bresc. 1602, 12mo.

"An Ancient Order of Knighthood, called the Order of the Band, instituted by Don Alphonsus, King of Spain, in the year 1368, from Cæsar Augustus, to wear a red ribbon of three fingers' breadth, and subject to xxxv. rules; the knights whereof were called by the same name:" first translated out of Spanishe into French by Don Anthonie de Guevare, and now Englished by Henry B. London, 1568, 8vo.

"A Chronicle of the Lives of Tenne Emperours of Rome, wherein are discovered their beginnings, proceedings, and endings, worthy to be read, marked, and remembered. Wherein are also conteyned Lawes of speciall profite and policie; Sentences of singular Shortnesse and Sweetnesse; Orations of great Gracitie and Wisedom; Letters of rare Learning and Eloquence; examples of Vice carefully to be avoyded, and notable Patterns of Vertue, fruitfull to be followed:" translated out of Spanish by Edw. Hellowes, Groome of her Maiesties Leashe, London, 1577. This Chronicle begins with Trajan and ends with Severus.

"Exegemata in Habacuc," auct. Ant. de Guevara; August. Vendel. 1603, 4to. The same under a different title, "Commentaria absolutissima et ecphrasis Antonii de Guevara in Habacuc prophetæ vaticinium;" Antw. Caspar Bellerus, 1609, 4to.

"A Book of the Invention of the Art of Navigation, and of the great Travelles whiche they passe that saile in Gallies," &c.: translated from the Spanish. London, 1578. 4to.

"Livre del Mont Calvaire;" Parti Prima en François, par Fr. de Belle-Forest, Paris, 1578, 8vo: Seconda Parte, Ven. 1560, 8vo; et Lat. Col. 1607, 8vo. "The Mount of Calvary: wherein is handled all the Mysteries of the Mount of Calvarie, from the time that CHRIST was condemned by Pilat until He was put into the Sepulcher by Joseph & Nichodemus," London, 1594, 4to. "Mount Calvarie; the Second Part. In this booke the Author treateth of the Seven Words of which CHRIST our REDEEMER spoke hanging upon the Crosse:" translated out of Spanish into English. London, 1594, 4to. "The First and the Second Part compyled by the Reverend Father Don Antonio de Guevara, Bishop of Mondonnedo, Chronicler and Preacher unto Charles the Fift," &c.: translated out of Spanish into English. London, printed by Adam Islip, for Edward White, and are to bee sold at his shop by the little north dore of Poul's, at the signe of the Gun. 1597.

The Second Part, on the Seven Last Words, was never completed by Guevara, as he died whilst writing it.

It remains to say a few words on the version presented to the modern Reader. The Translator, where practicable, has followed the old English rendering, but he has avoided as much as possible its archaism. The present is not to be regarded as an exact reproduction of Guevara's beautiful work. It was found to be too quaint, and even in many places too extravagant, to be profitable for devotional reading at the present day. In some parts of the book, also, a certain exaggeration of sentiment, and in others a repetition which is apt to become wearisome, pervades the original. All this has been omitted.

Often Guevara's meditations and explanations turn on a rendering of the Vulgate, to which the English Version does not lend itself. In such cases, a text which answers the purpose has been substituted, and the Bishop's words have been adapted to suit it.

Sometimes the Author touches on a most significant type or moral lesson without fully drawing it out. The Translator has ventured, in such instances, to add a few words, taking them chiefly from Mystic Writers of the same country as Guevara—from De Barzia, Osorius, or Luis de Granada.

Re-arrangements of the text have also been made. Occasionally, quotations suitable for one Chapter have strayed to places where they are without point. These have been restored to their proper position in the book. Towards the end of the volume, pages are filled with addresses of S. Joseph of Arimathea to the Blessed Virgin, and her exclamations of sorrow. These (which are not always written in the best taste) have been expunged; and suitable portions of the Prologue to the Meditations have been inserted to fill their places.

In preparing this English Edition of "The Mysteries of Mount Calvary" for publication, regard has been had to its object, as a book of devotional reading for the Season of Lent, and not as a mere literary curiosity.

QUINQUAGESIMA, A.D. 1868.

Contents.

CHAPTER		PAGE
I.	THE CONDEMNATION OF THE SON OF GOD	1
II.	THE PURPLE ROBE	6
III.	THE CROWN OF THORNS	11
IV.	THE REED	15
V.	THE BLOW WITH THE REED	19
VI.	THE SALUTATION	22
VII.	THE GENUFLEXION	28
VIII.	THE GARMENTS OF CHRIST	32
IX.	THE GARMENTS OF JOSHUA THE HIGH PRIEST	36
X.	THE CROSS-BEARING	41
XI.	THE KEY OF DAVID	46
XII.	GOLGOTHA	51
XIII.	SIMON THE CYRENIAN	55
XIV.	ON TAKING UP ONE'S CROSS	60
XV.	THE WEEPING WOMEN	65
XVI.	JESUS STRIPPED OF HIS GARMENTS	69
XVII.	THE THIRD HOUR	73
XVIII.	THE NAILING OF THE HANDS	78
XIX.	THE LIFTING OF THE CROSS	82
XX.	THE LOTS CAST	86

Contents.

CHAPTER		PAGE
XXI.	THE SEAMLESS ROBE	90
XXII.	THE PASSERS-BY	94
XXIII.	THE DARKNESS	98
XXIV.	THE LOUD CRY	103
XXV.	THE BOWED HEAD	106
XXVI.	THE RENT VEIL	110
XXVII.	THE RENT ROCKS	114
XXVIII.	THE OPENED SEPULCHRES	119
XXIX.	THE TESTIMONY OF THE CENTURION	124
XXX.	THE SMITTEN BREASTS	128
XXXI.	THE PIERCED SIDE	132
XXXII.	THE SPEAR	137
XXXIII.	JOSEPH OF ARIMATHEA	142
XXXIV.	JOSEPH AND NICODEMUS	147
XXXV.	THE DESCENT FROM THE CROSS	151
XXXVI.	THE TYPE OF JACOB	155
XXXVII.	THE ANOINTING OF CHRIST	158
XXXVIII.	THE RIGHT MAINTAINED	163
XXXIX.	THE ENTOMBMENT	167
XL.	CONCLUSION	170

THE MYSTERIES OF
MOUNT CALVARY

THE MYSTERIES OF MOUNT CALVARY.

CHAPTER I.

The Condemnation of the Son of God.

"HE delivered JESUS to their will," are the words of S. Luke (xxiii. 25), when speaking of the sentence of Pilate upon CHRIST, which is as much as saying, Seeing that Pilate the judge could not obtain of the Jews what he requested, he yielded the point, and condemned the SON of GOD to death, in such manner, that He should be subject to their will and pleasure. S. Cyril remarks, That Pilate gave no directions as to the manner of death JESUS was to die, but merely delivered Him over to the will of the Jews, that they might do with Him what they would, and revenge themselves upon Him as best they could; and Damascene says, in one of his sermons, That because Pilate delivered JESUS to their will, the Jews inflicted on Him as much as their malignant wills could devise.

It is tolerable, observes Origen, that accusers should deliver an offender to the judge; but, that the judge should hand over the accused to his enemies is a perversion of justice. When Pilate delivered CHRIST to their will, he proved himself an unjust judge; for no man ought to judge upon an accusation, but on evidence ; nor ought he to give sentence without hearing the defence; nor condemn the accused to be at the mercy of the accusers. For what else did these accusers desire but to put Him to death? And what death did they plan for Him but that of the Cross? O wicked Pilate! exclaims S. Chrysostom, seeing thou dost confess with thine own mouth that the SON of GOD was taken through envy, and is accused through malice, why dost thou suffer Envy to revenge itself on Innocency, and permit Justice to be suppressed by Malice?

S. Basil says, in commenting on the Psalms, That because unjust Pilate delivered CHRIST to their will, the Jews were bold to torment Him in many ways ; for, as He went through the streets, with their feet they spurned Him, with their hands they smote Him, with their fingers they plucked out His hair, with their spears they wounded Him, and with their tongues they blasphemed Him ; and, because they had licence to do according to their will, they left nothing undone that they could do.

Remigius observes, that at the time when CHRIST was delivered over to the will of the Jews, they might have let Him go, had they listed ; but because the SON of GOD had made choice to die on the Altar of the Cross, the judge was constrained to command, and they to execute the sentence.

O Good JESUS, Love of my soul, I appeal from Pilate's sentence! For if the judgment had been according to justice, the commandment would have been given, not to deliver Thee unto the Jews, but the Jews unto Thee. If Pilate had commanded them to follow Thy will, as he willed them to work their will on Thee, Thou wouldest have used great tenderness towards them; for Thou wouldest have pardoned them. Neither will I that Pilate give Thee over to my will, but rather deliver me to Thine. For if he deliver Thee unto me, I know not how to entreat Thee ; but if I am given over unto Thee, Thou knowest right well how to dispose of me. It is more wholesome counsel for us to put ourselves into the hands of GOD, than for GOD to commit Himself into the hands of men ; for He will take care of those whom He hath made, for whom He died, and to restore whom He arose from His grave.

It is worthy of observation, that Holy Scripture says, He delivered JESUS to their will, not to their wills. A multitude of people have generally a variety of opinions; but on this occasion they were of one heart. In matters touching virtue the wicked disagree, but in matters of sin they are of one opinion. And now these Jews are all of one wicked mind—agreeing to put CHRIST to death—agreeing to cry out, "Crucify Him! crucify Him!"—agreeing to ask for Barabbas to be released instead of CHRIST—agreeing to mock Him with, "Thou that destroyest the Temple, and buildest it in three days, save Thyself!" Indeed, their will was as one: for, excepting Pilate, who said, "I find no fault in Him;" his wife, who bade him "Have nothing to do with this Just Man;" and the thief, who said, "This Man hath done nothing amiss"—we read of none that laboured to do good to CHRIST, or made any resistance to the unanimous decision against Him.

What means this, O Pilate? Dost thou deliver CHRIST to such a perverse nation and perfidious people, and of such malignant will? Canst thou not bear their cries in thy ears? And how canst thou give Him over to bear their scourges on His shoulders? Is there any justice which doth command, or any law which doth ordain, that to avoid their tongues thou shouldst deliver Him into their hands? If thou didst so fear their tongues, thou shouldst have inquired into the causes of His accusation, and have declared openly the reasons why thou didst condemn Him. Verily, strange causes wrought in the mystery of this condemnation. The Jews accused through malice; thou didst condemn through fear; whilst JESUS died through love.

O Good JESUS, my soul's delight, who could have deprived Thee of life, without Thine infinite charity suffering it? Thy unspeakable love gives sentence against Thee. Thy goodness doth dissemble it. Thy humility doth consent that it should be so. Thy Divinity approves of it. Thy heart embraces it. Thy flesh endures it. My necessities require it. O Giver of Life, and Slayer of Death, who dare condemn Thee to die? O JESUS, condemned to death, am not I, perchance, he who doth accuse Thee, he who gave sentence against Thee? Mine is the guilt,

Thine is the condemnation. Life of my life, why dost Thou not close my life with Thine, seeing that this day Thy life doth end for mine?

Rabanus says, That Naboth was judged because he would not give his vineyard to king Ahab; Susanna was judged because she would not consent unto the elders; but CHRIST was judged because the priests bore Him great envy. And S. Jerome observes, That the indulgence of passion in a judge blinds him to justice. Thus the love of the elders condemned Susanna; and the hatred of the priests caused the death of CHRIST.

When the Jews said to Pilate, "We have no king but Cæsar," from that hour they transferred their allegiance from the GOD of Judæa to the Emperor of Rome, and lost a liberty which they valued, to incur a servitude which they abhorred. S. Augustine asks, With whom are they better off, with the GOD of Hosts, or the Cæsar of Rome? GOD gave them liberty to enjoy, captains to follow, priests to instruct them, laws to observe, a Temple in which to worship, Scriptures to comfort, a land to inhabit; whereas Cæsar, whom they now choose for their lord and king, will enslave them, murder their children, throw down their walls, burn their Temple, spoil their land, and sell them as bondsmen. Seeing that before Pilate you asked that CHRIST'S Blood should be on your heads, says Gregory Nazianzen, and that you submitted at the same time to a foreign prince, marvel not that this Blood pursues you, and that tyrants oppress you, O ye Jews! And S. Cyril follows in the same strain. After the unhappy Jews had said, "His Blood be on us," "We have no king but Cæsar," they have been trampled down of all the world, and have been always governed by strangers. And this curse will remain among them to the end of the world, because in CHRIST'S presence they renounced their liberty, and asked for vengeance on their deed.

It may be remarked in this place that there fell three fears at once on Pilate's heart, and fought within him at the same time; the first, the knowledge of CHRIST'S innocence: the second, the hearing Him declare Himself the SON of GOD; and the third, the threat that he would not be regarded as Cæsar's friend unless he consented to the people. But in the end Pilate resolved rather to give up CHRIST, than to lose the office he held. Had he remembered the words of Matthias, "Fear not the words of a sinful man: for his glory shall be dung and worms" (1 Macc. ii. 62), he would not have feared the threats of the Jews; for when a good man does that which the law commands and reason advises, he may be sure that though the wicked may contradict, they cannot overthrow. The number of the good is but small compared with the multitude of the ungodly; and were it not that this handful were under the constant protection of GOD, they would soon cease to exist. But He Who does not suffer a leaf to fall from the tree without His will, sustains the righteous by His power. Who dare say that our Blessed LORD cares less for the souls of His faithful than for the leaves of the trees?

Therefore we need have no fear, though evil men and seducers wax worse and worse; for we will not dread their wrath, nor feel alarm at their threatenings. There would not have been at this day a Saint or a Martyr in the Church of GOD, had they feared what tyrants could do to them.

The true servant of the LORD will not ask, What will be said of me? or What will be done to me? but, What will in the end become of me? Because it is not the hard words of man, nor his harder dealings, which destroy; but it is that which we do ourselves which decides our future condition. Far were these considerations from the mind of Pilate, when, for fear of man, he violated justice, yielded to malice, condemned innocence, and lost his own soul.

CHAPTER II.

The Purple Robe.

"AND when they had mocked Him, they took off the purple from Him, and put His Own clothes on Him," says S. Mark (xv. 20). Aulus Gelius and Macrobius tell us that, from the time of the adoption of Assyrian customs by the Roman court, the Emperor always wore a crown of gold on his head, a sceptre in his hand, a purple garment on his person, and was addressed with bended knee. Now, when the SON of GOD had confessed before Pilate that He was a King, although His kingdom was not of this world, Pilate's servants made merry over Him, because that He Who was weak in power, poor in wealth, simple in His answers, and mean in His knowledge, and altogether without favour in the eyes of man, should claim a regal position. And not only so, but because He declared that His kingdom was not of this world, did they the more despise Him. For Pilate and his soldiers thought nothing of that future life in which His kingdom was to be established; and they accepted His words as proof of His madness, and therefore jested and mocked CHRIST as though He were "stricken of GOD and afflicted." And so they made Him act the part of a king, and wear a garment of purple, and bear a thorny crown, and hold a sceptre of reed, whilst they bowed the knee to Him, saying, "Hail, King of the Jews!"

If CHRIST had said that His kingdom was of this world, then He might have seemed to have prejudiced the Roman commonwealth; but by saying that it was not so, He removed all excuse from Pilate for condemning Him, and for giving Him over to the mockery of the soldiers, and the will of the multitude. S. Anselm remarks, with great beauty, Pilate on his seat of judgment, and the thief in his bonds alike heard these words, "My kingdom is not of this world;" but to one they were the savour of life unto life, to the other the savour of death unto death; for Pilate laughed at the saying, and asked, "Art Thou a king, then?" whilst the thief pleaded, "LORD, remember me when Thou comest into Thy kingdom."

How sorely must the Good LORD have suffered in His soul from this unseemly mockery! It eases the pain we endure when we are treated with scorn, if we consider that we have deserved it by our fault. But the Blessed JESUS was guiltless. Men are wont to jest over those who have some moral or bodily blemish; but who dare say that in CHRIST was any spot? These soldiers in Pilate's court had no excuse for treating Him in the manner they did; for His person was beautiful, His conversation was holy, His doctrine was very truth itself, His words were circumspect, and His works were altogether good.

Mock not, O Pilate! exclaims S. Chrysostom; mock not at CHRIST, neither do thou consent that those of thy house scoff at Him, by clothing Him in purple; for there is in Him that which is not manifest to all, but which will hereafter appear.

Rupert, in commenting on S. John, quaintly remarks, The hatred of the wicked towards CHRIST was so great, that by their will they would have changed Him into another. They changed His skin when they scourged Him; they changed His garments when they mocked Him; they changed His estate when they crowned Him; they changed His name when they said, "Behold the Man!" they changed His family when they gave Him thieves for His companions; and they changed His life when they slew Him.

"Thou hast known My reproof, My shame, and My dishonour!" says the Prophet in CHRIST'S person (Ps. lxix. 20). It is as if He cried out, O My Eternal FATHER! Thou, and Thou alone, dost know and comprehend My humiliation, the internal shame and outward dishonour I endure, the reproof to which they put Me, the shame that covers My face, the dishonour of false witness borne against Me! Thou hast known

My reproof! because the injuries endured are so many, and the torments borne are so grievous, that mortal tongue could not rehearse them, and human mind could not conceive them.

A reproach, a shame, and a dishonour was that indeed, when the purple robe, a garment used for honour to clothe princes, was in dishonour placed on CHRIST. It was inflicting a species of martyrdom, doing such dishonour and offering such a reproach to CHRIST. The veil of the holy of holies was of purple; the curtains of the ark were purple; Mordecai, in mark of honour, was clothed in purple; in purple did the kings of Midian array themselves, for it was the colour held in highest repute, and regarded as a badge of honour. Shall the purple then lose its reputation, and be counted vile, because the SON of GOD was clothed in it in mockery? Why did GOD permit that there should be purple in the Temple of old, seeing that His SON should be vested in it before Pilate in mockery and scorn? Because that the poor purple covered the naked and wounded person of JESUS, shall it therefore lose its ancient repute? Nay, verily. In this clothing the Good LORD in purple is a mystery which was unperceived by Pilate's court, but which has been revealed unto the Martyr host.

"Thine head upon Thee is like Carmel, and the hair of Thine head like purple" (Cant. vii. 5), saith the Bride to CHRIST, as though she would say, When I behold Thee, whom my soul loveth, I see that Thy head is beautiful as Carmel, and Thy throat like a tower of ivory, and the colour of Thy hair is as it were a princely and fine purple dyed in the blood of the fish. The ancient Tyrian purple was made from the juice of a cuttle-fish, and the wool that was dyed was steeped in the purple blood in tanks. And by law no man was permitted to wear purple, unless he were a king, or of the blood royal. By the head which is like Carmel, is signified CHRIST the head of His Church; and by the purple is meant His precious Blood, and by the locks His glory; or, by the purple hair may be understood His Martyrs, who were dyed and made red with the blood that flowed from His scourged and bleeding back. S. Cyprian, in his Book of Martyrdom, says, What other meaning had that purple robe wrapping CHRIST, but the company of Martyrs which, throughout the world, embraces Him? What other meaning has this purple robe covering all His naked flesh but this, that He will accept the death of His Martyrs and clothe Himself with their testimony as an honour. This garment was first dyed in the blood of the fish, and then again in that which flowed from CHRIST, which teaches us that all our sacrifices, all our sufferings, all our works must be steeped in the sacred Blood of CHRIST to be made worthy.

By the Blood of CHRIST soaking the purple robe, dye was added to dye, colour to colour, painting to painting. And this was to make us plainly understand, that when CHRIST did bathe that purple in His own most precious Blood, He allowed and accepted all the blood that should afterwards be shed for Him in His Church. Theophylact observes, As the HOLY GHOST made Caiaphas say, " It is expedient for us that one man should die for the people," and Pilate to say, " What I have written, I have written," so did He make these men to put on CHRIST a robe of royal purple. For it is no other thing for the Blessed JESUS to be clothed in purple, than to be united to His Catholic Church.

S. Jerome declares that this garment, intended to do shame to CHRIST, became afterwards to Him great honour; for afterwards there was an infinite number of Martyrs who robed themselves in the same bloody purple, and gladly laid down their lives for His sake. O purple-red garment, happy purple! When was thy price and thy estimation so high? When wast thou elevated to so noble a position as that of covering the sacred flesh of Him under Whose feet the Seraphims cast their crowns? The Everlasting FATHER gives His Angels licence only on bended knee to adore His Eternal SON, Whom thou with thy folds dost cover. In past times thou, O purple, wast placed in honour on him who was destined to wear thee; but now He Who putteth thee about Him giveth honour unto thee.

O Good JESUS, wilt Thou not make a crimson garment of my stony heart, wherewith I may cover Thy mangled flesh, and then with that purple of Thine veil my wounded soul? Steep this heart of mine in Thy precious Blood, O LORD, that therewith empurpled it may be meet to cover Thee, and Thou to clothe me. Alas! my soul is more wounded with transgressions than Thy flesh is wounded with the scourge; therefore, O LORD, with the purple of Thy Blood be Thou pleased to cover me.

It is also to be observed, that whereas CHRIST in Pilate's hall was entirely robed in purple, yet the Canticle speaks only of His hair as being purple. This signifies that the LORD accepts good desires which proceed from the head, and which are figured by hair, as well as the intentions of the heart carried into execution, which are represented by the robe which covers the person. There are Martyrs in will as well as Martyrs in deed. S. Bernard writes thus: He is clothed in purple on whom the Blood of CHRIST is well bestowed, and then is it well bestowed when he conforms his life to the Gospel; for it avails him not that CHRIST shed His Blood for him, if he do not bathe his own life in that Blood. And he has his hair dyed purple who has all his thoughts drenched in the contemplation of the Blood of CHRIST.

CHAPTER III.

The Crown of Thorns.

"AND when they had platted a crown of thorns, they put it upon His head" (S. Matt. xxvii. 29). Doubtless it was a cruel mockery and a sore jest to place a thorny crown upon His head, as it were, to hedge about His head with thorns. If an old trodden thorn will wound the hardest heel, surely these fresh spines must have rent and hurt the tender temples of CHRIST. The ancient writers speak much of crowns given in reward for certain deeds ; crowns mural, triumphal, naval, civic, and military ; crowns of laurel, of oak, of vine-leaves, or of bay, but never of a crown of thorns. Those ancient crowns were all for honour, this crown alone was for dishonour. They all were rewards, this one alone was a punishment. The purple robe was a jest, the thorny crown was a torture ; for, as the thorns enter the delicate flesh, blood flows. At the pillar the leathern scourges drew the purple streams from His back. In the palace the thorns opened the veins of His head. S. Bernard supposes that the keenest sufferings of the Blessed SAVIOUR in His Passion were the Sweat of Blood, the thorny crown, the piercing of the nails, and the swooning of His Mother before His face. O Good JESUS, how well didst Thou pay Pilate for retaining Thee a little while in his house! For Thou didst hallow the greatest portion of it with Thy Blood, sprinkling therewith every gallery, porch, and hall.

"Moses took the anointing oil, and anointed the tabernacle, and the altar, and all his vessels" (Lev. viii. 10, 11). On the day upon which GOD commanded Aaron to be consecrated

High Priest, Moses anointed the altar, and all things pertaining to the tabernacle, with holy oil. Now these things were an allegory: for the altar is CHRIST, and the ornaments pertaining to it are His sacred members. But these were not anointed with oil: they were hallowed with the Blood that poured from His veins. And as Moses hallowed every vessel, so was CHRIST altogether bathed in His Own most precious Blood. And as on the same day that the altar was anointed Aaron was made High Priest, so also on the selfsame day that CHRIST anointed Himself did He assume the sovereign Priesthood over His Church. There was also this difference between the unction of the tabernacle and that of the Church, that Moses spent no more oil than would just moisten the finger; but, in the great Unction which our great Redeemer made of His Church, He expended all His sacred Blood.

Oh, what difference there is between seeing and describing, between speaking and tasting! Sad and woeful was the agony that CHRIST passed through in Pilate's house, when some stripped Him of His garments, and others clothed Him in purple; when some put a crown of thorns on His head, and others pressed it down upon His head, and others again placed a reed in His hand.

"Cursed is the ground for thy sake; thorns also and thistles shall it bring forth to thee," was GOD's sentence at the Fall. It was as though He had said to Adam, I blessed the earth when first I created it; but now that thou hast sinned, lo! I curse it, that it shall give thee brambles for wheat, and produce in abundance thistles and thorns, that thou mayest labour for thy food, and eat thy bread in the sweat of thy brow. According to the old law, moreover, the Cross and him who died on it were held to be accursed. But now that the Good LORD is content to wreathe His head with thorns, and to lie on the Cross as upon a couch, all is changed; the curse is removed, every thing is made very good once more, all things are reconciled, for all are hallowed with His most precious Blood.

S. Cyprian, in speaking of our Divine LORD'S Passion, observes, Our flesh was the thorn and thistle producing earth labouring under GOD'S curse. It is our flesh which brings forth continually the sharp spines which pierce our consciences and wound our souls. The soul is wounded when sin hath pierced it; and unless that thorn be plucked out, it will die. The earth of my own flesh is cursed. For, if I clear it of the brambles of pride, it bringeth forth the thorns of envy. If I weed out the nettles of covetousness, immediately up start the thistles of anger. If I root out the bushes of gluttony, straightway it produceth a crop of lust. And if it lie fallow for a single day, it becomes overgrown with the grass of sloth.

Theophylact thinks the thorns which pierce the conscience are the principal weapons of Satan; and he concludes, That the wearing of these thorns by CHRIST indicates Him as loading Himself with our offences. Why didst Thou suffer this crown to gird Thy temples, O my Good JESUS? How grievous must have been this wreath laid on Thee by cruel hands in Pilate's hall; but far more grievous is that crown of my sins and iniquities which I give unto Thee! Those thorns wounded Thee but for a day, whilst mine continually cause Thee to suffer. Abstain then from sinning, O my soul, for as many sins as thou committest, so many thorns dost thou weave into the crown of thy GOD.

S. Basil beautifully observes, This crown opened many fountains of Blood in CHRIST'S head; and the Martyrs, in pouring forth their blood for Him, prepared so many precious crowns for His brow. What were those stones which smote down S. Stephen, but thorns that took away his life and wove a glorious crown for his LORD? And, following out a similar idea, S. Augustine likens this crown to glory, and the spines to the Martyrs composing it.

But there is another mystery to be noted in this crown of thorns. CHRIST never wore a chaplet of roses, but only a wreath of thorns; whereby we are given to understand that, in the high rooms of the Church, those living delicate lives, like roses, should not be placed; but men who are penitent, austere, and severe, like thorns. If you desire to rest upon the head of CHRIST, and to have a place in His crown, make yourself a thorn of austere life, and in your adversities be patient. Under crowns of gold lie many cares, and a crown of thorns brings more pain still. O Good JESUS, I would that it should please Thee of Thine infinite goodness to give me this Thy crown, and if not, at least to impart to me some portion of it; for though I be not a king worthy to be diademed, yet am I a sinner deserving punishment; and though Thou wast most unjustly crowned, yet do I deserve justly to be mitred with the scroll of my offences. On Palm Sunday last, as Thou didst enter Jerusalem, the people strewed palm-branches in the way, beneath the feet of the ass on which Thou didst ride. They did more honour to the earth than these men do to Thy sacred head. O cruel thorns! I conjure you by that which GOD made you, pierce no more those holy temples, but come, rather, and transfix this stony heart of mine.

O Good JESUS, I do not ask of Thee, like Eve, that I should be given of a forbidden tree; nor, like Peter, that Thou wouldst take me with Thee into the ship; nor, like the sons of Zebedee, that I should sit at Thy side; nor, with the ruler, that Thou wouldst go with me to my house; but all I entreat for is, that Thou wouldst give me Thy crown for my pillow, and with Thine hand wouldst smoothe it for me. O my Redeemer, my LORD crowned with thorns! those thorns have been blunted in Thy head, and what were sharp once have now become very sweet. I fear them not; for the thorns of tribulation have been broken, and have blossomed into the roses of comfort. Suffer me, I pray Thee, Good LORD, if not to rest on Thy crown, at least to lie beneath its shade; and if there fall not to my lot the thorns that be on high, yet let me not fail to receive the Blood which runneth down, even to the ground.

CHAPTER IV.

The Reed.

"THEY put a reed in His right hand: and they bowed the knee before Him, and mocked Him, saying, Hail, King of the Jews!" (S. Matt. xxvii. 29). This was the third token of contempt and scorn offered unto CHRIST. The first was the purple robe; the second was the crown of thorns; and the third is this hollow reed. By the first they charged Him with pride; by the second they accused Him of ambition; and by this third they mocked His folly. Among princes their dignity is symbolized by the purple, their authority by the crown, and their justice by the sceptre. And to CHRIST a weak and hollow reed was offered as a sceptre, in token that His rule was without wisdom to deliver, and without strength to enforce, the justice He claimed to execute. Those injuries that were past touched His body; this affected His honour. But, exclaims S. Chrysostom, if this Man, into Whose hand is put the reed in token of the folly and weakness of His rule, be weak and foolish, then heaven and earth themselves will crumble away!

S. Jerome, in one of his Homilies, remarks; The words, "My kingdom is not of this world," cost our Blessed LORD very dear, for from the time that He said them He was reputed to be mad. But those words, "My kingdom is not of this world," signified this: O Pilate! CHRIST said, though thou seest Me sold as a slave, apprehended as a thief, bound as a madman, on My knees as a servant, accused as a malefactor, and witnessed against as one given to sedition, yet know that I am a King, and that I have a kingdom, though that kingdom be not of this world. S. Ambrose says, When the SON of GOD spoke these words, He undeceived the Jews who looked for a temporal monarchy, and He likewise let Pilate see that He did not aspire against Tiberius; but neither understood His signification, and both made a jest of the words spoken, and of Him who uttered them. Rabanus Maurus suggests that JESUS, by saying that His kingdom was not from hence, not only undeceived the Synagogue, but the Church as well; for He plainly gave her to understand that she must pass through much affliction in a world of which He was not the king. And S. Bernard pointedly asks, Why dost thou ask of Him a quiet life, much honour, great possessions, or good report? Ask them of the princes of this world, not of Him Whose kingdom is not in fleeting time, but in eternity.

This saying, which was a scandal to the Jews, to us Christians is full of comfort, remarks Theophylact; for by it CHRIST assured us that there is another kingdom whereof He is King alone in His Majesty, whence He descended to suffer death, for the purpose of raising us from this perishing and suffering world, to reign with Him in immortality. S. Cyprian eloquently exclaims, O Good JESUS, Thou sayest well, " My kingdom is not of this world ;" for if it were of this world, Thou wouldest not consent that the proud should dwell with the humble, the passionate with the patient, the covetous with the quiet, the carnal with the chaste, and the simple with the guileful. Into Thy kingdom enters no wicked thing, whilst in the world evil rules over the good. And again, S. Anselm very tenderly expresses himself on this subject: This speech of Thine Pilate's servants regarded as folly, taking it in jest; but I, O LORD, understand it in earnest; for I esteem myself only because I am Thine, and Thou sayest that Thou hast nothing in this world; then how can I desire any thing in this world? How dare I seek out any thing this world can give, seeing that He Who made it refused to make it His kingdom?

"They put a reed in His right hand." It is customary among men to regard the right hand with greater honour than the left, and consequently, we always place that person whom we most regard on our right hand. Thus Solomon seated his mother on his right hand; Moses saw the fiery law on GOD's right hand; Raguel married Tobias to Sara by the same hand; and S. Stephen saw CHRIST standing at the right hand of GOD. So also, at the last day, to the Right Hand of GOD will pass the elect.

S. Ambrose, in commenting on S. Luke, says, They made great jest over CHRIST'S assertion that His kingdom was not of this world, and they put a reed in His hand as a sceptre of justice; giving us to understand that, as the reed is barren, and is worthless in building, so did they esteem His kingdom, which was devoid of power and destitute of fruit. And S. Cyril observes, As the reed is tender and weak, and produces no fruit, therefore the servants of Pilate placed it in CHRIST'S hands as emblematical of His kingship, which was powerless to direct and enforce rule, and barren of advantage to His subjects. S. Jerome sees a further significance in the reed. According to him, it symbolized the old Law, which was hollow, dry, and fruitless; for it consisted only of the bark, which was the letter, and was devoid of the pith, which was CHRIST.

"Hollow with boards shalt thou make the altar," was the command given to Moses (Exod. xxvii. 8); that is to say, Moses made a tabernacle in the wilderness, in which was an altar on which to sacrifice, not made of stone, but of shittim-wood, and hollow. S. Gregory the Great affirms, That the altar of the old law was hollow and empty to signify that the synagogue was without the True CHRIST. Indeed, there is nothing solid and stable in this life, unless it be established and filled with GOD. All was hollow, all was empty, all was lifeless under the old Covenant; for those who lived under it possessed nothing substantial, but looked forward in hope.

CHRIST was given in His Passion vinegar, gall, and a reed— symbols of the treatment He received of the Synagogue. For it was keen as vinegar, having degenerated from the wine which was in the beginning good; it was bitter as gall in its malignity; and it was hollow as the reed, empty of all grace and virtue, making professions, but without practice.

But in the right hand of the SON of GOD, the hollow reed of the old Law became sound and firm, when for the letter He gave the Spirit, for the prophets He gave Apostles, for sacrifices

Sacraments, for the old Covenant the New Testament, for the figure the Truth, for a hollow altar a sound Gospel. Was not the Mosaic Law a dry and hollow reed, when, at its best time, the Law and the Synagogue broke down and fell to the ground? Origen says, that in the old tabernacle the boards of the altar were more valuable than the altar itself; but in our Sacred Altar, which is CHRIST, although the boards of His sacred Humanity are very perfect and good, yet His most glorious Divinity is better.

O Good JESUS, Love of my soul, why dost Thou take into Thy hand a hollow reed, when my sinful soul is nigh? This poor soul of mine is as the reed dry through lack of devotion, hollow through want of charity, fruitless in good works. She bears leaves only—the fluttering leaves of idle words. My sorrowful soul is a dry and hollow reed, having through carelessness and wilfulness fallen from Thy grace, and lapsed into Thy disgrace; dry though rooted in the weak and watery ooze of this fleeting world, moved with the first wind of temptation, broken at the first touch of tribulation. Leave then, O Good JESUS, leave that dry reed, and take this my hollow and empty soul; and in Thy hand she will become firm through the strength which Thou impartest, and full of the pith of charity Thou wilt impart, and her leaf will not wither, but she shall bring forth her fruit in due season.

CHAPTER V.

The Blow with the Reed.

"THEY smote Him on the head with a reed," says S. Mark (xv. 19), which is as much as saying that, not content with a jest, they wounded Him in earnest. For the SON of GOD to suffer Himself to be crowned with thorns, was indeed marvellous; but to suffer a reed to be placed in His hand, and then to yield that reed to His tormentors to be converted into an instrument of torture, is not merely to be wondered at, but is also to be feared.

O wonderful obedience, unspeakable patience in the SON of GOD! Let Thy torments cease, O Good JESUS, for Thou hast already suffered enough to replenish heaven and rob hell of its prey! But no; the sin of my soul is so great, and so often repeated, that it necessitates a prolongation of His pains.

"They have been a staff of reed to the house of Israel. When they took hold of thee by thy hand, thou didst break, and rend all their shoulder: and when they leaned upon thee, thou breakest," said GOD by Ezekiel (xxix. 6, 7), threatening King Nebuchadnezzar; that is to say, When thou, O King of Egypt, shouldst have been as a strong staff whereon My servant Israel might have stayed himself, then thou didst prove thyself but a hollow reed that breaks and casts him who leans on it to the ground, therefore will I inflict on thee judgments many and grievous. Our Blessed LORD commends the Baptist because he was not such a reed swaying in the wind. We may then conclude, that the reed in Holy Scripture represents him who has no stability, and no strength of purpose; him, in short, upon whom no reliance can be placed.

Agmon, in his Commentary on S. John, observes That every Christian in name who does not walk worthy of his profession, is like a reed, which has bark but not core.

It is worthy of note that CHRIST was thrice offended with the reed, whereas with the spear He was hurt but once. And so is it in the world; those who afflict the SAVIOUR most are they who in name are Christians, but who in fact are continually doing Him violence. Once was CHRIST mocked with the reed, when it was put into His hands; the second time He was smitten with it on the head; and the third time it bore the vinegar and gall to His lips. He who is a hypocrite is the man who puts the reed into CHRIST'S hand, his life being, like the reed, productive of the leaf of words alone, and having a void heart within. He smites CHRIST on the head with the reed, who is a heretic, and falsifies the truth. And he gives CHRIST the reed with vinegar and gall, who offers Him works, yet remains obstinate in sin. The wine of good works is there, but it is mingled with the gall of unrighteousness.

It is the property of the reed, however small it may be, to waver in the wind—a meet image of those who have no constancy in that which is good, and offer no resistance to that which is evil. Not a vice knocks at their gate, but straightway they open to it; not a desire presents itself, but they fulfil it forthwith. Are not those hollow reeds who remain upright so long as no blast of temptation blows, and give way at once to the slightest breath of the enemy?

Venerable Bede says with justice, That to wound the head of CHRIST is to assail His Divinity, and that those who deny the Godhead of CHRIST are they who strike Him on the head with the hollow reeds of their perversions. And Rabanus, following out the same idea, says, That to strike Him on the heart is to deny His knowledge; to strike Him on the eyes is to dispute His power of seeing all things; to smite Him on the feet is to declare that He doth not pervade all space; to bruise His hands is to assert that He doth not provide all things; and to strike Him on the head is to deny that He is LORD of all. But perhaps it will be nearer the truth, if we say that the blow dealt Him on the head comes from the denier of His Divinity, and that he who rejects His Humanity pierces His heart.

Damascene says That those strike CHRIST on the head who set themselves to judge and search out the inscrutable judgments of His wisdom, and who, with their philosophy and vain deceit, after the tradition of men, after the rudiments of the world, intrude into those things which they have not seen, not holding the head; wherefore they often rudely draw forth His Blood to their condemnation, when it should have flowed for their redemption.

Theophylact asserts, that as often as men neglect to do a good work, having time and opportunity for doing it, they do repeatedly strike CHRIST on the head; and that he who is slothful in the business of saving his soul, is ever drawing forth the Redeemer's Blood.

When I consider, says S. Hilary, how empty of virtues I am, like a reed, there falls on me great sadness of spirit; but when I remember that CHRIST did not disdain to take that reed in His hand, I revive, for the SON of GOD is He Who alone can fill my emptiness, and fulfil me with His goodness.

CHAPTER VI.

The Salutation.

"HAIL, King of the Jews!" said Pilate's servants to CHRIST (S. Matt. xxvii. 29) when they had clothed Him in purple, had put a crown upon His head, and set Him on a throne, and given Him a sceptre. But this they did, not to honour Him, but to do Him dishonour. The deeds they did, and the words they used, sprang all from a perverse intent. The words they spake were well enough; but the motive which prompted the servants of Pilate to speak them were evil. It is ever so with the wicked; they may do that which appears right, but seeing that the motive cause is evil, the act is thereby vitiated. "Woe to the wicked," says the Prophet; "it shall be ill with him!" (Is. iii. 11)—that is to say, Woe to him whose heart is corrupt, who is set upon wicked desires and plotteth that which is evil, and regardeth not that which is good; for though for a season all things prosper, yet in the end it will indeed "be ill with him." To bow the knee to CHRIST was right, to salute Him with Hail! was also right, to call Him King was well done; but, inasmuch as the bent knee and the salutation proceeded from malice, and were done in mockery, they became mortal sin. Hence learn how that an act which may appear right, an act done in accordance with GOD'S law, may still deserve GOD'S vengeance. "Man looketh on the outward appearance, but the LORD looketh on the heart" (1 Sam. xvi. 7). This is the difference between the judgments of man and the judgments of GOD. Men estimate the quality of a work by its outside show, but GOD weighs the inward intent of the soul. For

The Salutation.

"all the ways of a man are clean in his own eyes; but the LORD weigheth the spirits" (Prov. xvi. 2).

My brother, says S. John Damascene, observe the unspeakable excellence of the SON of GOD, which is declared not by His disciples so much as by His enemies. Pilate wrote, "JESUS of Nazareth, the King of the Jews," and nailed it on the cross as His title. Caiaphas said, "It is expedient that one Man should die." Pilate's wife said, "Have thou nothing to do with this just Man." The servants said, "Hail! King of the Jews." The centurion exclaimed, "Truly this was the SON of GOD." For His goodness was of such force that it constrained not only the good to acknowledge it, but the wicked to confess it. S. Cyril observes, The accursed Jews stop their ears when Pilate says to them, "Shall I crucify your King?" and when the servants hail Him as "King of the Jews;" for they would not have this Man to reign over them, but yielded themselves as bondsmen to a foreign tyrant.

It was not without mystery, that when CHRIST was in the cradle the Wise Men asked, "Where is He that is born King of the Jews?" that on His entry into Jerusalem the people cried out, "Blessed be the King that cometh in the Name of the LORD!" that the servants of Pilate should salute Him with the same royal title, and that Pilate should nail that title to His Cross. You lie, O ye Jews! exclaims S. Augustine, you lie in saying "We have no king but Cæsar;" for in the house of Herod the title of King is given to CHRIST; it is given Him also in the hall of Pilate, and all Jerusalem greets Him as King. Pilate confesses that He is a King. Why then do you deny Him the kingdom, and refuse to accept Him as your Anointed One?

When JESUS saw that the people would "take Him by force, to make Him a King, He departed into a mountain Himself alone," says S. John; for He fled from that position to which, as SON of David, He was entitled. And, because we may draw one mystery out of another, it is to be noted that the SON of GOD never gainsaid those who called Him a King, and yet He never consented to their making Him a King, thereby giving us to understand that He did not forsake the dignities and honours of the world because they did not belong to Him by right, but because it was His will to be without them.

S. Hilary on this point says pertinently, When the SON of GOD is called a King, and yet refuses to be made King, He gives us to understand that the estate of Kingship was His by right, but that He despises it. For he is more honourable who deserves rule and possesses it not, than he who acquires it without right. It is a greater mystery than at first appears, that CHRIST should submit to be called King, and yet refuse to be a King; and thus our Good LORD acted, to the end that His Godhead should be acknowledged and His humility should be observed. For, by the salutation of King, He was indicated as One Who was more than what He seemed to be; whilst, by His refusal of the kingdom, He gave example of that humility which He preached to others.

When CHRIST fled the kingdom offered Him, He betook Himself to the mountain-top to prayer. If Thou wouldst give me the choice of these two things, O Good JESUS, I should rather be with Thee in prayer on the mountain, than reign without Thee in Galilee.

What doth it avail thee, O my soul, that thou renouncest earthly dignities and pomps, if thou goest not up into the mountain of contemplation, there to abide in prayer with JESUS? Ascend, O my soul, into the mountain with CHRIST, following the evangelic life; for the perfection of the servant of the LORD consists not in desertion of the world, so much as in the virtues acquired in Religion.

If thou say, my Brother, that thou hast no rule or kingdom to forsake, let it suffice thee that thou hast a will to despise; for, in the house of our LORD, it is more esteemed to overcome the will in its perverse affections than to set light on our worldly possessions.

"Behold," said Joshua, "the LORD of all the Earth passeth over before you;" and Hosea says in GOD'S Name, "I will go and return to My place."

We may place these passages together, and see from them the King passing from the Synagogue, not stationary in the midst of it. The MESSIAH was to go before His people, and, being rejected by them, was to leave them till they should say, "Blessed is He that cometh in the Name of the LORD!" He Who was promised by the Prophets is as one on a journey, making as though He would go further; and the Synagogue lets Him depart without following Him, as did the disciples of the Baptist when they beheld Him walking, and as the disciples at Emmaus, who bade Him tarry with them, for the day was far spent. A King is He, but a King Who values not this earthly kingdom, and Who shares that which is in heaven with men, aye, even with thieves and harlots! For to the thief who asked to be remembered when CHRIST entered into His kingdom, He promised a share in it that day; and to the Jews He said, "Verily I say unto you, that the publicans and the harlots go into the kingdom of GOD before you" (S. Matt. xxi. 3).

S. Cyril observes, CHRIST did not say in vain to the Jews, "Search the Scriptures;" for they testified to His Kingship as GOD, and to His rejection of the kingdom as Man. And indeed these Scriptures would have shown them how that He Who was their MESSIAH should come to His own and be not received of them; how He would then "pass over before them," and, leaving them, "go and return to His own place." O wicked Synagogue, O unhappy Jerusalem! seeing that, according to the prophet Hosea, CHRIST would go from thee, and, unrecognized of thee, return to His own place, behold thy house is left unto thee desolate. He came to thee, and thou didst not know Him; He entered thy house, and thou wouldst not receive Him; He gave thee His doctrine, and thou wouldst not believe Him; He spake unto thee the things of GOD, and thou understoodest Him not; yea, He died for thy liberty, and thou wouldst not accept the oblation.

Compare with the words of Hosea those spoken by CHRIST to His Church: "Lo, I am with you always, even unto the end of the world" (S. Matt. xxviii. 20). From the Synagogue He passes away, that He may abide with His Church. "I will go," He says, "from thee, O Synagogue, to which I did come meek and lowly, from thee who wouldst not have Me, to a people whom I have not known, but whom the LORD shall choose, to a chosen generation, a royal priesthood, a peculiar people; and this shall be My rest for ever; there will I dwell even unto the end of the world."

O Good JESUS, I most humbly beseech Thee to stay and look upon my sinful soul, pass not by too speedily, for I am Thy creature, the work of Thine hands, though I be the least and most unworthy of Christians. What doth it avail me that Thou passest before my eyes, if Thou tarry not to wipe away mine offences? Stay, then, LORD JESUS, stay a little while in my heart, to the end that, if Thou shouldst call, I may open; if Thou shouldst speak to me, I may understand; if Thou shouldst instruct me, I may take Thine instruction to heart; if Thou shouldst counsel me, I may follow Thy counsel; if Thou shouldst desire me, I may learn to desire Thee!.

But to return to the salutation, "Hail, King of the Jews!" Hail! that is, GOD save, the King of the Jews. They who will put CHRIST to death ask GOD to save Him! How can these two exclamations, "Hail, King of the Jews!" and "Crucify Him, crucify Him!" be made to agree? How can the same fountain send forth at the same time sweet water and bitter? How ask in one breath Pilate to slay CHRIST, and GOD to save Him? It is a habit of evil men to use good words without intending good by them. Their words may be smoother than oil, and yet be they very swords. They sue that they may entrap; they salute to deceive; they promise that they may betray; and they flatter with their tongue, but their throat is an open sepulchre. With this word Ave! Hail! Joab saluted Amasa; and at the same time embracing him, he thrust him through with a dagger.

With this word Ave! the Mother of GOD was saluted by the Angel, and the SON of GOD was mocked. In the Angel's mouth it was hallowed, in those of the ministers of Pilate it was profaned. With this word Ave! Judas betrayed his LORD in the garden. With this word Ave! CHRIST saluted His disciples after His resurrection. Thus the word which is good and life-bearing in the lips of one, is full of evil and death in the mouth of another—and that a word full of good in itself. But holy words in the mouths of the wicked are profaned, as pearls that are cast before swine.

The Salutation.

Ave! Hail! With this word was the Incarnation announced, and it was the witness of the Resurrection. Ave! Word of good repute! seeing that the Angel pronounced it, the Virgin heard it, the Heavenly FATHER sent it, for His SON was it delivered, and the Catholic Church preserves it.

CHAPTER VII.

The Genuflexion.

"THEY bowed the knee before Him," says S. Matthew (xxvii. 29), meaning that, as Pilate's servants had it in their hearts to make good earnest of their jest, having enthroned CHRIST, and saluted Him with their lips as a King, they did Him homage also with their bodies.

It is to be noted, that those who are wicked and bent on malice, are ready to abase themselves to the vilest acts and to give their persons all kinds of toil and travel, if only they may accomplish the object of their malignant wills; but they will not exert themselves to lift a straw, where good may ensue. These servants would have counted it too great a trouble to have brought a cup of cold water to moisten His parched lips; but they regarded not the labour of plaiting thorns, of cutting a reed, and of bowing the knee.

" I have sworn by Myself, the word is gone out of My mouth in righteousness, and shall not return, That unto Me every knee shall bow, every tongue shall swear," said GOD by Isaiah (xlv. 23), that is, I have sworn by Myself, and have determined in My eternal wisdom, that none shall open his mouth but to confess Me, none shall bow the knee but to worship Me.

To understand this aright, we must observe that the three Wise Men fell down and worshipped CHRIST; that the Apostle declares that he bows his knee "to the FATHER of our LORD JESUS CHRIST;" that Daniel kneeled three times a day; that the leper came kneeling to our LORD, as did also he who had a lunatic son; that, in like manner, the woman with the issue of blood fell down before Him, worshipping Him; and that Simon Peter did the same at the feet of JESUS. And we read in the Apocalypse that the four-and-twenty Elders that are before the throne fall on their knees to worship the LAMB. We may gather from these examples that in Holy Scripture the bodily reverence of the bent knee is dedicated to GOD. And this outward genuflexion is to be united with the devotion of the heart and the praise of the lips. It is to be weighed, that GOD is not satisfied with the bowed knee alone, but with the praise of the tongue as well; nor is He satisfied with the bent knee and the words of homage only, for these did the servants of Pilate render Him, but with the devotion of the heart to prompt the outward acts. GOD would rather have men praise Him with their tongues and not kneel, than kneel and not praise Him; and He would prefer to both the drawing nigh unto Him with their hearts. But that worship is most perfect and acceptable which has its source in the heart, and which finds its utterance in words, and its expression in reverence.

Those in Pilate's house bent the knee, and blasphemed Him. They did not honour Him, but mocked Him; they did not confess Him, but denied Him. Rabanus Maurus says That in Holy Scripture the word "Ave" was hallowed and dedicated to GOD to praise Him withal; so likewise were the knees dedicated and hallowed to worship Him, and the hearts to love Him: but these ministers of wickedness with their Aves blasphemed Him, with their knees mocked Him, and with their hearts abhorred Him.

All hypocrites are disciples of Pilate's servants, for they bow the knee before men, yet bear false witness against their brother at the same time. They hurt the head of CHRIST whilst saluting Him; for whilst in profession they are bowed at His feet, in practice they are smiting His head. S. Bernard writes, With those of Pilate's household, those men blaspheme CHRIST on their knees, who, whilst kneeling in the Church of GOD, suffer their minds to range over evil things; for they serve CHRIST with their knees, but with their thoughts they spit on Him.

"I bow the knee of my heart, beseeching Thee of grace.

I have sinned, O LORD, I have sinned, and I acknowledge mine iniquities," was the prayer of Manasses, a captive in Babylon, which we may paraphrase thus: O Mighty GOD of Israel, my offences have been many and great, more than "the sands of the sea;" and instead of amending, my transgressions were multiplied, I heaped fault upon fault, and now, in my misery, I acknowledge how grievous they are, and beseeching Thee to pardon me, I bow to Thee the knee of my heart.

Understand, my brother, that to bow the knee is to acknowledge a fault; that when thou art prostrate before thy Maker, then thou art amending, and as token of amendment thou art giving evidence of humility. The unbending knee is a token of pride and obduracy; the bowed knee is a token of humility and of a softened spirit.

Yet what doth it avail thee to bow thy knee to the ground, if thy sin stand upright on foot? If thou wilt serve the LORD thy GOD, and if thou wilt pray, like King Manasses, from thine heart, thou must first cast down to the ground all thine offences, before thou bendest the knee; for the LORD hears most readily those who pray with a clear conscience, but He shuts His ears to the obdurate heart, however prostrate the body.

See an example of this in the hall of Pilate. The servants on bowed knee obtain only their condemnation, and lo! the thief standing wins Paradise. For he bowed the knee of his heart, they only that of the body. Then the servant of the LORD bows the knee of his heart, with King Manasses, when he amends his faults, and inclines his heart to forgive injuries; but then is it rigid, when he will not pardon his enemy, nor flee his sin, but rather vaunts himself in defending it, than seeks to amend it. S. Jerome says, that however bad it may be to sin, it is worse to persevere in it; and it is worst of all to defend sin when committed, for then amendment is furthest off.

If through good desires Everlasting Glory was to be won, who so sure of it as thou, O my soul? What virtue or what goodness is there this day in heaven or earth which is not desired of my eyes, wished of my heart, and asked of my tongue? I desire to be holy, I desire to be just, I desire to be good, I desire amendment; but, woe is me! other men occupy themselves in good works, and I only in vain desires. What greater folly is there, or what vainer hope, than to heap sin upon sin, and to defer repentance till old age? He bows his right knee to the ground, who leads a righteous life in all but one respect, the forgiveness of an injury. And he bends his left knee, who is so good-natured as to pass readily over any trespass committed against him, yet will not leave the sin which doth so easily beset him. But he is a true servant of the LORD, bowed on both knees, whose body is occupied in honest employment, and whose heart is occupied in holy thoughts, insomuch that he can say with the Apostle, "I live; yet not I, but CHRIST liveth in me."

Manasses did not say, I bow the knee of my body, but, the knee of my heart; whereby he gives us to understand, that it will avail us little if we bow these material knees, if those of our soul remain rigid. For our LORD takes more account of one thought of the mind than of the disposition of our members. Oh, how many there be in this world, who in Church kneel on both knees, and yet are stiff at heart. What are the knees that the heart must bow, but the Will and the Nill, stubborn knees not given to relax. If sinful Manasses does not venture to pray without first bowing that stubborn will and nill, tell me, I ask you, how dare you address GOD, without first bowing thy likes and thy dislikes into submission to His holy pleasure?

Take heed, therefore, my Brother, take heed, and do not prostrate thyself like Pilate's ministers, who served CHRIST on their knees, but blasphemed Him with their tongues. Do not, then, appear unto men to be a saint, at the same time that thou art so sensitive to the least insult, so full of presumption, so destitute of humility.

CHAPTER VIII.

The Garments of Christ.

"THEY took off the purple from Him, and put His own clothes on Him," says S. Mark (xv. 20); that is to say, when the servants had mocked CHRIST to their heart's content, and Pilate had condemned Him to death, they drew the purple robe from His shoulders and put on Him the apparel in which He had been taken. It is to be observed, that CHRIST was clothed with three garments on the night of His Passion—that which was white, in which Herod arrayed Him; another of purple, in which He was vested in the house of Pilate; and another of scarlet, in which He was exhibited to the people with the words, "Behold the Man!"

S. Jerome says, In this is the malice of His enemies, and the patience of the SON of GOD made manifest, that during His life none gave Him a coat, but in the hour of His death they mocked Him with three; from which we may see how much more liberal men are in matters of jest, and folly, and profanity, than they are in charitable concerns.

"My Beloved is white and ruddy!" exclaims the Bride (Song of Solomon, v. 10). It is as if she said, O daughters of Jerusalem, my true Bridegroom, my one well-beloved Friend, has His face white as snow, and His cheeks blooming as red roses. Lo! are not these the colours which CHRIST wore in His Passion—the white, and the scarlet or crimson? the white in Herod's palace, the crimson and purple in that of Pilate. And S. Bernard, commenting on the passage in Solomon's Song, says, Not without a great mystery is the Bridegroom praised of the Bride for being white and ruddy, and is He arrayed in white and in purple-red; for these colours symbolize—the white, the chastity of His Virgins, and the red, the blood of His Martyrs. What else does this attire signify, but the Saints which CHRIST hath in His Church? He hath as many garments to clothe Himself withal as He hath just ones in His Church. Until Constantine the Great, CHRIST was chiefly attired in crimson, because until then the Church suffered persecution, and there were many Martyrs; but from thenceforth He vests Himself in white, for now is the age of Confessors and Virgins. " Wherefore art Thou red in Thine apparel, and Thy garments like him that treadeth in the winefat? I have trodden the winepress alone" (Isa. lxiii. 2, 3). Thus speaks the FATHER to the SON, and thus answers Him the Incarnate WORD. It is as if the Eternal FATHER asked, Tell Me, O My Beloved SON, why is Thy vestment so red, and of so crimson a dye? and for what reason is it like the garment of one who trampleth grapes in the press? And the SON answered, Because I not only planted My vineyard, O My FATHER, but I alone gather My grapes, when the vintage is come, and I alone stand in the vat when they are trodden; therefore is My garment stained, and My flesh empurpled.

It is to be observed, that the garments of CHRIST were not dyed at the time of planting or of pruning the vine He brought out of Egypt, but in the crushing of its grapes. It was not under the old Dispensation that He was reddened with His Blood, but then when He was severing the juice from the vine, that is, the Church from the Synagogue. And the dye which stains the garments of the treader of the press leaps up from that which He tramples under foot. Thus was the blood which empurpled the robe of CHRIST drawn forth by those malignant enemies whom He placed under His feet. When He pressed upon them with His preaching and example, then they boiled up against Him. S. Cyprian says, The SON of GOD feared not the Jews, but made small reckoning of them. He reprehended them in His sermons, and unveiled their hypocrisy, and they rose from under His feet, not only to hinder His preaching, but to bereave Him of life. In separating the husk of their vices from the good wine of virtue, then did CHRIST steep His garments in blood. Rabanus remarks, For the SON of GOD to say that His garments were red, was because He alone on the Cross trod the grapes beneath His feet; that is, the garment of His Humanity was soaked in the red dye of His Blood, through the sour grapes of our offences which He crushed beneath His feet.

Had there been no grapes in the vat, then had not His garment been stained. Had there been no offences in the world, then would not the SON of GOD have died. Speaking figuratively, we may say that the vine is the Church, the grapes are the faithful, the press is CHRIST'S Passion, the beam is His Cross, and the treader is CHRIST.

O my soul, look well to thyself, that, if the Good JESUS should tread thee down with tribulation, or wring thee with temptation, there leap not out of thee some drop of blasphemy and impatience wherewith thou mayest befoul the garments of thy LORD. How wouldest thou that the dross of sin should depart from thy soul, as long as thou remainest in pleasure and indifference? The husk must be separated from the juice, and that can alone be done by the crushing of the grape. If the most blessed Soul of the SON of GOD did not leave the rind of the body without His flesh having first been wrung and trodden, how wilt thou that the offence of thy soul should leave thee without suffering and bruising. Then, O my soul, permit thyself to be wrung in the hands of thy Creator, and crushed by the foot of thy Redeemer; for as the wine that makes glad the heart of man has to be crushed from the grape before it can be quaffed, so must thou be tempted and tried before thou art meet for the banquet of Eternal Life.

"I have trodden the wine-press alone," says CHRIST; for He, and He alone, trampled the grape in the vat, and of the people there were none with Him. He, and He alone, can tread out the evil and elicit the good.

Carry me, O Good JESUS, is the prayer of S. Bernard, carry me to the place of Thy Passion, and put me in the press of correction, and thus separate the gold from the dross, the rose from the thorn, the juice from the grape, the sin from my soul.

I have had no pity in trampling on Thee, O fear not Thou to bruise me.

"Pharaoh sent and called Joseph, and they brought him hastily out of the dungeon: and he shaved himself, and changed his raiment, and came in unto Pharaoh" (Gen. xli. 14). After the innocent Joseph had interpreted the dreams of the chief baker and butler, and was remembered by the latter, his apparel was changed, and he was brought to the king. In none of the patriarchs do we find so distinct a type of CHRIST as in Joseph. As Joseph was cast into prison because he would not commit adultery with his mistress, so the SON of GOD was condemned to death because He would not yield to the errors of a wicked and adulterous Synagogue; on which account He was set between two malefactors on the Cross, as Joseph in prison was set betwixt two criminals. One of Joseph's companions was condemned to die, the other was promised life; and so was it with the thieves who suffered with CHRIST on the Cross—the one was condemned, the other was saved.

But Joseph "came in unto Pharaoh" in changed apparel; that is to say, CHRIST laid aside mortality to be clothed in immortality, He left behind His weakness to be girded with strength, when, on the Ascension-day, He entered into the presence of the Eternal FATHER, no more in feebleness, no more in sorrow, no more in pain, but "glorious" henceforth "in His apparel," and "clothed in majesty and honour."

CHAPTER IX.

The Garments of Joshua the High Priest.

"HE shewed me Joshua the High Priest standing . . . . clothed with filthy garments . . . . before the Angel. And he answered and spake unto those that stood before him, saying, Take away the filthy garments from him . . . . and I will clothe thee with change of raiment" (Zech. iii. 1. 3. 4). This vision of the Prophet is full of mystery. It is to be understood of CHRIST JESUS, and of no other. The name Joshua is the same as JESUS, and means a Saviour. And He Who is our SAVIOUR, is our Great High Priest as well. Wherefore, we Christians may rejoice, in that we have a Saviour Who can deliver us, and a Priest Who can absolve us, One mighty to defend us, One ever standing, watchful to preserve us. S. Stephen, like Zechariah, beheld JESUS standing, not sitting; for "He that keepeth Israel shall neither slumber nor sleep" upon His guard. Happy indeed may we be, and grateful to our LORD, seeing that we have a Saviour to watch for us whilst we sleep, to bear the pain that we may rest, to fast that we may eat, to stand that we may sit, to extend His great care over us, caring little for Himself! I speak this, O Good JESUS, to extol Thy power and to give Thee glory; for without Thee to watch for me, without Thee to defend me, I should be caught of my enemy the devil.

It is to be noted that of Joshua the High Priest it is said. "Is not this a brand plucked out of the fire?" By which figure of a burning brand we are to understand CHRIST in His two

The Garments of Joshua the High Priest.

Natures—the wood of the Humanity united to the fire of the Divinity.

The Abbot Rupert, commenting on this passage, says, That the HOLY GHOST could not have given us a fitter symbol than this firebrand. For in the burning brand the fire is so united and transformed with the wood, and the wood with the fire, that the same substance is at once wood and fire. So in the Hypostatic Union, CHRIST our SAVIOUR is True GOD, and true Man, joined into One. Before He was incarnate, He was all Fire; but since He took flesh, He became a burning Brand. "I am come to send fire on the earth; and what will I, if it be already kindled?" And He is a Brand "plucked out of the fire;" that is, He, and He only, has no smoke of sin, no fault whatever. For the fire shall try every man's work of what sort it be, His only excepted, which needs not to be tried, for it alone is very good. From the fire of original sin, wherein all the world was burning, only this holy Firebrand escaped being scorched and smoked. The fire of pride came not nigh Him, nor the coal of envy, nor the smoke of anger, nor the flame of lust, for He was not overcome of sin, but sin was conquered by Him.

Oh, high Mystery! Oh, unspeakable Sacrament! The SON of GOD having escaped an universal fire, falleth into another and a greater fire; for though the furnace of sin did not consume Him, yet the flames of love embrace and kindle Him; and, O my soul, behold Him held up on the Cross, a light to lighten the Gentiles, a beacon on the top of a mountain, burning in the ardour of His consuming love.

"Joshua the High Priest was clothed with filthy garments," says Zechariah. This figure literally applies to CHRIST; for the white robe given Him by Herod, and that of purple in which He was arrayed by Pilate, were the oldest, the most ragged, and the foulest that could be found. For the tormentors sought not to do CHRIST honour, but to heap on Him dishonour.

Rabanus declares, that the Jews laboured more to defame CHRIST than to torture Him; they sought rather to destroy His honour than His life. For this cause they made Him a companion in death of thieves, that He might be regarded as a malefactor; they clothed Him in ridiculous garb, that He might be accounted as mad; they witnessed against Him that He was a rebel, that He might be disgraced. And S. Cyprian says, For thirty years CHRIST was in the world and was not molested, because He did not then bear testimony against it; but as soon as He preached and rebuked evil, then the Scribes and Pharisees, perceiving that their credit was at stake, resolved on taking away both His life and His reputation. To which S. Augustine adds, The object of those who put a crown on CHRIST'S head, a reed in His hand, a purple-red mantle on His person, was to discredit Him. They sought but one torment to take away His life, but many torments to destroy His reputation. And Theophylact observes: The vesture was threadbare, to impair His credit; torn, to rend His doctrine; foul, to stain His life. Yet these garments were not His own: in clothing Him in other men's apparel, they imputed to Him the sins of others.

But leaving the letter, and searching out "what the Spirit saith unto the Churches," we discover that in Holy Scripture garments are used to symbolize lives and conversations. Thus the Psalmist speaks of the wicked man who "clothed himself with cursing, as with a garment," and of being "covered with dishonour;" so, on the other hand, Job says, "I have put on righteousness, and it clothed me;" and Isaiah, "He covered me with the robe of righteousness." And CHRIST says, "Blessed is he that keepeth his garments, lest he walk naked;" and "He that overcometh shall be clothed in white raiment;" and of the Bride, "To her was granted that she should be arrayed in fine linen, clean and white; for the fine linen is the righteousness of Saints." When GOD bids us keep our garments clean, He means us to be chaste, and to keep ourselves unspotted from the world; He exhorts us to keep our Baptismal innocency, lest we walk naked—that is, destitute of the innocence and grace given us at the Font. "Let them cover themselves with their own confusion, as with a cloak," says David. Man puts on that cloak, when he pursues the way of perdition, and hardens his conscience, and blinds his eyes to shame. Cassidorus, commenting on this

Psalm, says, Thou dost so often cover thyself with confusion, as thou dost sin against GOD.

The garments we wear, then, in Holy Scripture signify the works we do. O Good JESUS, how can my tongue rehearse, how can my pen write concerning the garments wherewith the ministers of Pilate clothed Thee? What other signification had the clothing of the High Priest in foul raiment, but the laying upon Thee, O JESUS, the iniquity of us all? The garment of Thy Humanity, which Thy FATHER made Thee, which the HOLY GHOST wove for Thee, which Thy Mother gave Thee, was made without sin, and presented to Thee without spot; but now Thou dost put on Thee my pride, my anger, my envy, my gluttony, my lust, and even my punishment. Thou didst array Thyself in all my offences and faults, as old and spotted garments, and didst wash them in Thy Blood, and make them white and clean. "He took upon Him the form of a servant, and was made in the likeness of men; and being found in fashion as a man, He humbled Himself and became obedient unto death, even the death of the Cross," says the Apostle, writing to the Church at Philippi.

S. Bede says, that the Apostle does not say that He took the likeness of flesh, for that would have lent a colour to those heretics who declared that He had but a phantom body; but that He was made in the likeness of men—that is, that He was like man in all points, sin only excepted. He took not on Him the nature of sin, but the likeness of a sinful nature. He was True GOD and true Man, a Redeemer, not a sinner. In the likeness of sinful flesh He was, seeing He took our sins upon that flesh and nailed them to His Cross with Himself. He was found in fashion as a man. Just as a man wears a garment to do him honour, CHRIST did wear our sins, but only to His humiliation.

There is also a mystery in the fact, that CHRIST took the garments that were given Him in the palaces of Pilate and Herod, and they were old, foul, and ragged. But the garment of Virgin Flesh given Him by His Mother He had before received, and that was new, pure, and whole. For thirty-three years did He wear that one garment, and now for less than three hours He wears the others. O Thou that clothest the heaven with stars, the deep with waters, and the earth with trees, why dost Thou abase Thyself to take garments of tyrants? If these be old, ragged, and foul, is not my soul aged in its wickedness? Is it not rent with many sins? Is it not stained with much transgression? Take Thou then my soul, O LORD, and wrap Thyself in it.

S. Bernard remarks: For the SON of GOD to take garments from His holy Mother, and also from sinful tyrants, is to the intent that we may learn that He receiveth all who come to Him, and despiseth none. The works of the good CHRIST taketh, that He may reward them; and the works of the wicked He taketh, that He may amend them. And S. Basil says: That our LORD took more garments from Pilate and Herod than He did from His Virgin Mother; for He would have us understand that there are more sinners than righteous, and that the sins wherewith He is offended are more than the services which are rendered unto Him.

Of the garments given Him by Pilate and Herod, CHRIST took none away with Him; as He received them in the palace, He left them there. By this we are to understand that we are to suspect all the favours of the wicked; and when we are in the company of those who are the enemies of GOD, to be careful to carry away from their society no evil habit, no bad counsel, no moral contagion.

Let us, then, leave Herod his white robe and Pilate his of scarlet; for thereby we are taught to forsake the pomps of the world. Agamon pithily remarks, that, as the SON of GOD neither brought these gay garments into the palace nor took them away, so is it with us. We brought nothing into this world, neither shall we carry any thing out. And yet the SON of GOD did leave the world with that about Him wherewith He entered not in—the wounds of the scourge, and the bruises of the blows He had received; and we, when we depart, shall go forth with the marks of many a grief and many a sorrow, and bruised with many a fall.

CHAPTER X.

The Cross-bearing.

"AND He bearing His Cross went forth into a place called the place of a skull, which is called in the Hebrew Golgotha" (S. John xix. 17). Divested of the gorgeous robe, and wearing His own raiment, the SON of GOD went forth with the Cross upon His shoulder towards the place called in Latin Calvary, and in Hebrew Golgotha.

No sooner had the judgment of Pilate been given, than the adversaries of CHRIST uttered a shout of joy and victory; and, may be, there was not one in all that rabble who did not seek the death of CHRIST with malignant hate.

GOD promised the Jews, by Jeremiah, "to make their land desolate, and a perpetual hissing; every one that passeth thereby shall be astonished, and wag his head" (xviii. 16). It was as if He said, Thy enemies, O Jerusalem, shall not be content with burning thee, and destroying thy Temple, overthrowing thy walls, robbing thy treasury, and imprisoning thy children; but, the better to mock thee, and show their joy over thy fall, they will shoot out their lips, and hiss, and clap their hands at thee.

How is it possible to expound these lamentable words without tears? Let not Jeremiah weep over the captivity of his people, but let us wail for the sentence pronounced upon CHRIST. Strangers take the people from their land, and this people bereave their King and GOD of life. That which the Assyrians dealt on the Jews, the Jews retaliate on CHRIST.

The Assyrians laughed over the destruction of Jerusalem: the Jews rejoice over the fall of their MESSIAH.

When the SON of GOD was condemned to die, some went in quest of wood, whereof to make a cross; others sought a carpenter to shape it: others, to dig the pit into which it was to be planted; others, to seek nails for the fastening of the SAVIOUR on it; and others, again, laboured to stir up the passions of the people. And, although by reason of the offices they had undertaken, they were dispersed through the city and separated from one another, yet they were all at one, and of one mind, touching the death of CHRIST. Long before the Crucifixion was carried into execution, CHRIST had been crucified in the hearts of His murderers.

When a man departs from this world, some go to prepare his grave, some stay to shroud him. These ministers of wickedness before CHRIST'S death in like manner took offices on themselves, but only to slay Him.

There is much to be weighed in this matter, and do thou, O my soul, weep; for if these wicked men lead thy LORD and GOD to shame, is it, thinkest thou, for His own fault or for thine? Thine is the fault, O my soul, and His is the punishment; thine the crime, His the bearing of the penalty; thine the life, His the death; thine the prize, His the purchase; thine the glory, His the strife. Be not absent in that hard and bitter passage. Accompany thy GOD in that sorrowful way, and join thy fault to His innocence, and lade thy sins on His precious members; for, woe unto us, if, when they lead Him to death, they take not away with Him the burden of our grievous offences.

The reason why they took the purple garment from the innocent Lamb, and clothed Him in His own raiment, was that all might recognize Him again; for He was so disfigured by the tortures He had undergone, that, but for the seamless robe, the torturers supposed He would not have been known again. But how do you suppose, O cruel men, that He shall not be distinguished from the two thieves? Hath He not a greater cross than they? Weareth He not a diadem, though of thorns? Watereth He not the streets with His Blood?

S. Bernard, in a sermon, preaches: Seeing that the blessed JESUS has His shoulders mangled by the scourge, His face befouled with spitting, His eyes bruised with blows, His hair thin through plucking, how should He not be known, seeing among all He is so distinguished for mocking?

S. Bonaventura, in his Stimulus, observes: O Good JESUS, tell me, I pray Thee, what favour did they render Thee in that palace?

They gave Me a heavy cross, laden on My shoulder; thieves they gave Me as companions, a halter round My neck, a crown of thorns on My head, bruises on My face, a crier on My left hand, an executioner on My right hand.

Thou hast told me, O JESUS, what Thou didst bring out of the palace, tell me now, I pray, what Thou didst leave behind?

That which I left in Pilate's house, was My hair strewn on the pavement, the floor bespattered with My blood, My skin cleaving to the garments which they put upon Me.

"They came unto the brook of Eshcol, and cut down from thence a branch with one cluster of grapes, and they bare it between two upon a staff" (Numb. xiii. 23). Spies had been sent by Moses to examine the Promised Land; and Caleb and Joshua, having walked through Canaan, and viewed the cities, in order to animate the Israelites by an evidence of its fruitfulness, cut a cluster of grapes and put it on a staff, and the bunch was so heavy, that it was as much as two men could bear.

The Land of Promise signifies felicity; the bunch of grapes symbolizes CHRIST, with the skin of His Humanity and the juice of His Divinity; the two men bearing the grapes are the Jew and the Gentile, taking CHRIST to His death on the staff of the Cross. And what did it signify, that in the day in which the spies carried the bunch of grapes into the camp of Israel, GOD was more wroth with the chosen people than at any other time; but that, on the day whereon CHRIST was taken to His death, the elect people committed their greatest trespass, and incurred the intensest anger of GOD? And as one spy turned his back on the cluster, whilst another faced it, so, in the day of CHRIST'S death, did some, like the bad thief, turn their backs on Him, to their condemnation; whilst some, like the penitent thief, looked towards Him to their salvation.

S. Augustine gives this interpretation of the type: What are the two spies that carry the grapes hanging on the staff, and resting on their shoulders, but the Jew and the Gentile leading CHRIST to His death? Of these two, he that went before, was the Jew, who turned his back upon CHRIST, and would not believe in Him; and he who went behind, was the Gentile, who had Him before his eyes to worship, insomuch that from that time the Church remained to be blessed with holy Jacob, and the Synagogue abides mocked with Esau. As the first-fruits which the Israelites saw from the Land of Promise was the fair cluster of grapes, so the first jewel from the lot of our inheritance is the person of CHRIST.

Who, asks Theophylact, is the grape-cluster hanging on the shoulders of the spies, but the True SON of GOD weighed between two loves? The one love was that which He bare to His FATHER, to satisfy Him; the other was the love He bare to us, to redeem us; and with the grape of His body hanging on the wood, He bought us and satisfied the FATHER.

Rupert the Abbot writes: Not without a mystery does the Scripture say where the bunch was cut, and who carried it, but does not tell who ate it; for it leads us to infer that the Jews plucked this most precious Grape of the body of CHRIST, and bound it to the staff of the Cross, and pressed it with their malignant hate; but who drank of that fruit of the True Vine? Not they, but a people whom they had not known; and, indeed, in this world it never will be truly known who taste of that wine and live, and who will drink of it at the Marriage Supper of the Lamb.

Oh, how happy are we Christians! Without having planted the vineyard, or gathered the grape, or pressed it in the wine-vat, we do yet receive the wine through the Sacramental channels, whilst the Jews taste not of it. On them is the sin of CHRIST's death, to us its fruits. That Grape on which the Jew tramples crowns the Angels. O holy and blessed Grape! we praise Thee, we worship Thee; for from Thee was wrung the wine which did redeem the world.

That Grape, which might have been to the wealth of the Jews, became to them an occasion of falling. That they did not rejoice and give thanks for the rich cluster which was brought to them in the desert, was a figure of the small advantage they would draw from the death of CHRIST; and hence it comes to pass, that the grape-cluster which was pressed in the Synagogue has sent its blood into the chalice of the Church.

But to return to the Via Dolorosa, and to CHRIST being led to death between the thieves. It may be that the Jews, by giving Him these robbers for company, would have the people suppose Him to be a robber; and, indeed, they accused Him of theft—for they said that He had committed the greatest theft of all, in stealing the Name of GOD, by calling Himself His SON, and in stealing the name of Cæsar, by calling Himself a King, and in stealing the name of Moses, by making Himself the giver of a new law.

O Good JESUS, what a change of degree is this! Thou, Who art served in heaven by Angels, Who didst accompany Thyself on earth with Apostles, dost now go through the streets of Jerusalem with thieves. Who accompanies thieves, but thieves? Who but Thou, O Good JESUS, hast stolen the essence of Thy FATHER, the innocence of Angels, the wisdom of the HOLY GHOST, flesh from men? Art Thou a thief, Who takest the letter to give the Spirit, the figure to bestow the Truth, prophets to send Apostles, the synagogue to endow the Church? The Paradise Thou didst take from Thy FATHER, unto whom didst Thou first give it, but to the thief upon the cross? O happy robberies! seeing that all that Thou didst take Thou didst return with usury. Take, Oh, take from me, then, this heart of stone, that Thou mayest give unto me a heart of flesh!

CHAPTER XI.

The Key of David.

"AND the key of the house of David will I lay upon His shoulder; so He shall open, and none shall shut; and He shall shut, and none shall open" (Isa. xxii. 22); that is to say, The love I bear to My Only-begotten SON, saith GOD, and the confidence I have in Him, are so great, that to Him alone do I commit great King David's key, the which He shall not bear in His hand, but on His shoulder; and that which He shall open therewith, none shall be able to shut; and that which He locketh therewith, none shall be able to undo.

The better to expound what this key signifies, we must refer to the history of King David.

David led a life of double character: he was happy, great, glorious; he was also sorrowful, afflicted, poor. We will not speak of him returning in triumph from the slaughter of Goliath and the Philistines, or as son-in-law to the king, captain of the host, victorious in battle, or reigning over GOD's people; but of David persecuted by his brethren in the camp, pursued by Saul his king, mocked by Michal his wife, scorned by Shimei his friend, fought against by his neighbours the Ammonites, rebelled against by his subjects—ay, by his own son Absalom.

But not only was David persecuted and afflicted, he was also very poor. Of Jonathan he took clothes, and of Abimelech he borrowed bread; he asked for milk and cheese of Nabal the Carmelite, and took grapes and figs of Abigail; and from Saul he stole a bottle of water. Among the afflicted he was most afflicted, and among the poor he was the poorest.

The Key of David. 47

When Gabriel the Archangel promised of CHRIST, that "The LORD GOD shall give unto Him the throne of his father David," and Isaiah, that on CHRIST should be laid "the key of the house of David," it was signified that the SON of GOD should inherit the afflictions and poverty of David. By the key is meant the Cross in which His sufferings culminated, and by the throne is meant strait poverty. To say that on CHRIST should be laid David's key, was to tell us that to Him was committed David's trouble; and to say that to Him was given David's throne, was to let us understand that CHRIST inherited his want and necessities. David had two heirs—Solomon, to whom was given the inheritance of kingdoms, and the SON of GOD, Who received that of his travail and trouble. Solomon and CHRIST are brothers in blood, but not in inheritance; for to Solomon it fell to be rich, to CHRIST it fell to be poor; to Solomon came peace, but to CHRIST came war; to Solomon descended the crown, to CHRIST the key; Solomon inherited the throne of dominion, CHRIST the seat of misery; Solomon became a king, CHRIST took upon Himself the form of a servant.

To what end, O Good JESUS, dost Thou marry Human Nature to Thy Godhead, seeing that Humanity brings Thee as a dowry only a strait seat and a heavy key? Thou art given no house in which to dwell, and yet Thou possessest a chair on which to sit; Thou art given no coffer, and yet Thou possessest a key!

Albertus Magnus says, Of all that David had in his palace, CHRIST inherited nothing but a heavy key and a narrow chair. And these are one; for that chair is His Cross on which He sat to die, and that key is also His most holy Cross wherewith He did open the Kingdom of Heaven to all believers. What was it for Isaiah to mean by saying that upon the shoulder of the MESSIAH should be laid the key, but that the SON of GOD should carry on His back the Cross, on His way to Calvary?

It is to be noted also, that they did not command Him to bear the key of His Cross upon both shoulders, but upon one only, whereby we are to understand that the SON of GOD bore the death He did suffer, not on the right shoulder of His Godhead, but on the left shoulder of His Manhood.

S. Jerome exclaims, We have never heard or seen a key, however heavy, which a man could not carry in his hand; yet this key was so weighty that it might only be borne on the shoulder, it was made heavy with the iron of our offences; and so heavy was it therewith, that beneath the weight the SAVIOUR fell, and it crushed the soul out of His body.

O holy and glorious key, that opens Heaven and shuts hell; that opens the Church and fastens the synagogue; that opens Sacraments and shuts the bloody sacrifices; that opens the sense and shuts the letter; that discloses grace and locks out sin!

S. Augustine comments thus on the passage: For Isaiah to say that what David's key opens no man can shut, and that what it shuts none can open, is to assure us that the mysteries which CHRIST wrought upon the cross, and shut up under the key, are so high and incomprehensible, that none can reach to them without He reveal them. So to the Apostle Paul He opened, with this key, when he saw Paradise and heard unspeakable words, which it is not lawful for a man to utter; so to S. Stephen He opened, when he beheld CHRIST standing at the right hand of GOD; so to S. Peter He opened, when he cried out, "Thou art the CHRIST, the SON of the Living GOD;" so also to the centurion He opened, when he exclaimed, "Truly this was the SON of GOD!"

O my heart, if thou desirest to enter into bliss, why dost thou not seek Him to Whom is committed the key to Bliss? The key of vice is kept by the vicious, the key of the world is kept by worldlings, but the key of Heaven is in the possession of CHRIST. O Good JESUS, seeing Thou art the Way that leadeth to the Door, and Thou the Door that admitteth to Bliss, and Thine the key that openeth the Door, and Thine the Mansion to which it giveth access, and Thou the Glory of that Mansion, why dost Thou not open to my poor soul, that is weary with calling after Thee? O Redeemer of my soul, O Sweetness of my life, didst Thou not say that Thy coming into this world was to save sinners? Lo! am not I a grievous sinner? Open Thou to me who knock!

But to return to the Way of Sorrows.

As the Jews had a great desire to see JESUS crucified, they laid on Him the instrument of His death. They desired to kill Him by force; and He, like a second Isaac, willing to die, went through the midst of them bearing the wood for the sacrifice.

Pilate had given CHRIST over to the will of the Jews. JESUS was led forth between the thieves who were to bear Him company; the procession was formed, the executioner walked on one side, the crier on the other, and the crowd followed. The cross was laid upon Him, and He went forth bearing it. Now does ambition trample on humility, anger tread down patience, covetousness triumph over charity, and the lie rear itself above the truth.

Because these wretches esteemed the SON of GOD as the greatest of thieves, they laded Him with the greatest of crosses, longer than the others, ruder wrought, and more weighty; this is S. Bernard's opinion. And so, as the SON of GOD went along the street, the crier began to cry, but not to proclaim the miracles of CHRIST, but the false witness that had been brought against Him; for the imperial magistrate had condemned Him as a deceiver of the people. And some looked out of the windows, others hasted to their doors; some hung about the street-corners, listening to the voice of the crier, and wondering that on the eve of so great a Sabbath, when criminals were wont to be released, a procession of death should move to the place of execution. Tongues are loosened against CHRIST as He passes along, and He hears the hiss, and the scoff, and the shout of rage—This mad fellow, this deceiver, this carpenter's son, this miracle-worker by Beelzebub's aid!

They have sharpened their tongues like a serpent: adder's poison is under their lips. Hide me from the gathering together of the froward, and from the insurrection of wicked doers; who have whet their tongue like a sword, and shoot out their arrows, even bitter words; that they may privily shoot at Him that is perfect; suddenly do they hit Him, and fear not. Wherefore, O Good JESUS, art Thou so cruel to Thine own Humanity? Why dost Thou hide Thy Godhead? Wherefore dost Thou, the Judge of all, allow these false tongues to judge Thee?

It is the opinion of an ancient Father that CHRIST suffered more torment at hearing so many wicked men blaspheme His honour, than at the sentence of Pilate on His life; for that pierced only His body, whilst this went down into His very soul.

But why boastest thou thyself, thou tyrant mob, that thou canst do mischief? Thy tongue imagineth wickedness; and with lies thou cuttest like a sharp razor. Thou hast loved to speak all words that may do hurt, O thou false tongue. Therefore shall GOD destroy thee for ever; He shall take thee, and pluck thee out of thy dwelling, and root thee out of the land of the living. But I became a reproof among all Mine enemies, but especially among My neighbours, whilst they of Mine acquaintance were afraid of Me, and they that did see Me without conveyed themselves from Me—Me, Who heard the blasphemy of the multitude on that awful day, shalt Thou, O My FATHER, hide in Thine own Presence from the provoking of all men, and keep secretly in Thy Tabernacle from the strife of tongues.

CHAPTER XII.

Golgotha.

"HE went forth into a place called the place of a skull, which is called in the Hebrew Golgotha" (S. John xix. 17).

It is worthy of remark, that oftentimes the Catholic Church leaves foreign words in their original tongue, untranslated; and when she does so, those words are full of hidden meaning and sacred mystery. Of such nature are the words CHRIST, Amen, Apostle, Hosanna, Bethsaida. These words are left in their original form; and though the meaning of some of them may be given, the Church retains the words themselves as full of matter deserving of meditation. Take, for instance, such a word as Amen, that signifies Truth; or Apostle, that may be translated Sent; or CHRIST, that signifies Anointed; yet, notwithstanding, they have a higher signification, and a greater depth of meaning in the original in which they were written, than can be rendered by a translation. The Evangelist, then, seeing the wonderful mysteries contained in the word Golgotha, or Calvary, has retained the two words—the one Hebrew, the other Latin; thereby giving us to understand that the name was more full of mystery than could be expressed, and that by thinking on it, we shall be led on to that which the sense requires, and not remain content with what the letter sounds.

Considering, then, Golgotha or Calvary, we see that either signifies the place of a skull; and we observe further, that the Hebrew and the Latin names are given, for both Jew and Gentile are included in the sentence of death which passed on all men, for that all have sinned. CHRIST in the garden prayed,

Abba, FATHER! in two tongues, for He reconciled to the FATHER Gentile and Jew. So here, on the hill of the skull, He becomes the Head and chief Corner-stone, joining together in one those who had long been separated.

Calvary was a place outside of Jerusalem, where thieves, traitors, and murderers were executed; and, as in course of time their bodies fell from the gibbets, they littered the mount with their bones. The hill was as a dunghill; for on it were cast the refuse of the people to decay, abhorred of all.

And this foul and loathsome spot was chosen by the SON of GOD as a fitting place in which to do battle with Satan! Where but on this charnel-house of Golgotha did the KING of Life and the King of Death encounter and slay one another? Here on this dung-heap, Satan bereft CHRIST of life, and CHRIST despoiled Satan of his power. S. Anselm says, It is a great and incomprehensible mystery, to see the SON of GOD die. But it is not enough to know He died; we must know, further, the cause why He died, which was man's offence; the company amidst which He died, which were thieves; the death which He died, which was infamous; when He died, which was in the prime of life; and where He died, which was among the loathsome sepulchres of Golgotha.

Prosper, in his Sentences, says: The Blessed JESUS would not die in the city, but without it; to give us to understand, that it is those without the city of His Church and the walls of the Faith that crucify Him. And S. Bernard adds, For the SON of GOD to die on the dung-heap of Golgotha, and not in the clean market-place of Jerusalem, was to let us understand that it is not in clean and pure souls that He suffers—in them He lives; but in the foul and festering hearts of sinners, dead in their trespasses, He dies. Origen traces a resemblance between CHRIST on Golgotha and Job on his dunghill. Job, he says, lay on the dunghill, sore with boils, and CHRIST was stretched on Golgotha full of leprosy, the leprosy of our sin which clave to Him.

O great goodness and infinite charity of the SON of GOD! Job in his misery "took him a potsherd, to scrape himself withal;" and CHRIST, covered with the disease, the wounds, and bruises, and putrifying sores of our sins, broke the golden bowl of His most precious heart, and the pitcher of His body at the fountain of His love, and with the fragments swept our offences away.

S. Hilary observes pertinently, That as man had sinned through all his senses, CHRIST must suffer in every sense. S. Augustine has the same thought. He says, Our first parents sinned in hearing when they gave ear to the serpent; they sinned in seeing, for they saw that the fruit was good for food and pleasant to the eyes, and, seeing, they lusted after it; they sinned in touch, for they plucked the fruit; they sinned in taste, for they ate of it; and they sinned in smelling, for they smelled the fragrance of the fruit. In atonement for these sins the Second Adam suffered, in hearing reproach, and blasphemy, and false witness; in sight, by beholding Himself encompassed with enemies, and by the tears He constantly shed; in touch, for all His nerves were wrung; in taste, when the gall touched His lips; and in smelling, when He was brought to this mound of corruption, Golgotha. S. Basil, commenting on the words of the Psalmist, "He taketh up the simple out of the dust, and lifteth the poor out of the mire," says, Of all the things we see, there is nothing more vile than a refuse-heap, and yet Job on one was most honoured and favoured of GOD, and CHRIST on one performed His greatest miracles; for in that place of death the Prince of Life conquered Death, and in that great grave of bones He robbed the grave of its prey.

"It came to pass, as they were burying a man, that, behold, they spied a band of men; and they cast the man into the sepulchre of Elisha; and when the man was let down, and touched the bones of Elisha, he revived, and stood up on his feet" (2 Kings xiii. 21).

The mysteries of this type are to be deeply considered. For one who is alive to raise another who is dead, happens sometimes; but for one dead man to raise another dead man is most exceptional. Without all doubt, Elisha, the prophet of the Old Covenant, was a good man, but the Elisha of the New Covenant is much better. In the time of Elisha none dare call the Creator any thing but GOD only, nor man any thing but human only;

but our Elisha unites the Godhead with the Manhood, is very GOD and also very Man. S. Augustine says, That as the prophet Elisha was able to raise one dead man to life when he was dead, so the SON of GOD by His death caused our resurrection. Elisha raised one only, whereas JESUS CHRIST will raise all. Elisha raised one who died after him, but JESUS raises those who died after and those who died before. S. Ambrose continues the comparison and contrast. Elisha raised one, yet remained dead himself; but the Blessed JESUS did at the same time raise Himself and raise me; He became alive again, and I awoke with Him. Rupert says, That the raising of the dead began with Elisha and was perfected with CHRIST; Elisha raised another, himself remaining dead; but CHRIST rose Himself in His true body, and at the same time raised the body mystical of His Church.

To come then to our purpose: not without high meaning did JESUS go to die on Golgotha among the bones of malefactors, because He, a true and better Elisha, went there to restore them all to life. O Good JESUS, on the Altar of the Cross Thou didst unweave the web of Thy Humanity, to weave again the web of my life. Who will be with Thee on that charnel-heap of Golgotha, to be raised by Thy hand? O Good JESUS, behold me dead and obstinate in sin; do Thou extend Thy power to me, and from this Golgotha of death raise me to a life of righteousness!

Go forth, O my soul, go, and walk by the sepulchres of Golgotha! Now it savoureth not, save of good; now it killeth not, but raiseth to life; now it supporteth not malefactors, but Martyrs; now there be no gibbet on it, but a banner; now no scattered bones, but justified sinners!

CHAPTER XIII.

Simon the Cyrenian.

"AND they compel one Simon a Cyrenian, who passed by, coming out of the country, the father of Alexander and Rufus, to bear His Cross" (S. Mark xv. 21).

S. Anselm, in his Meditations, says, Now the murderer Cain carries his brother Abel into the fields to slay him; now Joseph is sold by his brethren; now Moses goes with his rod to open the Red Sea; now also Jacob leans upon his ladder to scale the heavens; now the Spies bear the heavy grapes hanged upon a staff; now Joshua the captain lifts up his spear against Ai; now Gideon holds up his sword over Midian; now Delilah hands over Samson to his enemies; now David launches his sling-stone at Goliath; now Jonah spreads out his hands to swim in the cruel waters; now Isaac bears the wood for the sacrifice upon his shoulders; now Noah builds the ark of refuge; now Esau bends his bow against the beasts of the forest; and now also Moses hangs the serpent in the air for the healing of the people.

S. Augustine comments thus: Because the way to Calvary was long, and the SON of GOD already very weary, the Jews, fearing lest Pilate should repent, or that the people should take Him from their hands, hired Simon of Cyrene, coming out of the country, to bear CHRIST'S Cross to Calvary; but this they did, not out of pity, but through their eagerness to see Him die.

Not without mystery does Scripture say who this Simon was, what he was called, and from whence he came. He whom the

Jews hired to carry the Cross was a Lybian, and a Gentile, not a Jew. For the Cross was so odious to a Jew, that none would have taken it on him at any price. So they forced this stranger to bear it. They were full of scruple over touching the Cross themselves, but had no scruple in crucifying their LORD. They scrupled to enter the palace of Pilate, but not to raise false witnesses. They scrupled to bear the Cross, but not to make it. Thus did they make the Word of God of none effect by their traditions.

S. Bernard exclaims, O Good JESUS, Redeemer of my soul, how is it possible for me to recall Thee on Thy way to Calvary without weeping? He who would have seen Thee on Thy sorrowful way, would have seen Thee stripped of Thy garments, bathed in sweat, sighing with weariness, falling beneath Thy burden, bruised with the weight, stumbling with weakness, dripping with blood.

In all that journey to Calvary, what other office had the Cross of CHRIST, save that of oppressing Him with its weight, galling His shoulders, thrusting against His thorny crown. The Jews urged Him forward, CHRIST strained Himself with the Cross, the Cross pressed the thorns into His head, the thorns rent His flesh, His flesh distilled the blood; and so He fainted through lack of strength, of breath, and of blood.

O my soul, why dost thou not go forth without the gate to meet thy LORD, and take His Cross from His shoulder, bearing His reproach?

In the forty-eighth chapter of Genesis is an account of the blessing of the sons of Joseph, Manasses and Ephraim, by the dying patriarch Jacob. Joseph set Manasses the first-born on the right side, and Ephraim the younger on the left; but his father's eyes "were dim for age, so that he could not see," and he stretched out his hands and, crossing the arms, laid his right hand on the head of Ephraim, and his left hand on the head of the first-born. "And Joseph said unto his father, Not so, my father: for this is the first-born; put thy right hand upon his head. And his father refused, and said, I know it, my son, I know it: he also shall become a people, and he also shall be great: but truly his younger brother shall be greater than he, and his seed shall become a multitude of nations." There are high mysteries contained in this figure.

What is signified by the blind Patriarch, but the blind synagogue? "Some of the Pharisees said unto Him, Are we blind also? JESUS said unto them, If ye were blind, ye should have no sin: but now ye say, We see; therefore your sin remaineth" (S. John ix. 40). It is to be noted, says S. Jerome, that the youth Manasses did not lose his eldership until his grandfather was altogether blind. By which we are to understand that the Children of Israel should not altogether lose their inheritance till blindness had happened to Israel. What greater blindness could there be than to deny the kingdom to the SON of David? What greater blindness than to give life to the murderer Barabbas, and to slay the LORD of Life? What greater blindness than to purchase the Blood of CHRIST with money, and to apply it to themselves in vengeance? What greater blindness than to scruple at entering Pilate's court, and not to recoil from crucifying CHRIST? Truly the Jews come from a blind father, seeing they act as blind men!

Jacob crossed his hands on his breast as he took the blessing from the elder and gave it to the younger. So, with the Cross committed to Simon the Cyrenian, passed the blessing from the Jew to the Gentile. The Jews seek out the Cross, buy the Cross, fashion the Cross, give the Cross to JESUS, and He bestows it on the Gentile Simon. Had they known that with the Cross was transferred to the Gentile all the treasures of GOD'S grace, they would not have been so glad to have seen it given to the Cyrenian. But as they were all children of the blind, what they did, they did blindly. Jacob, without seeing, made a cross with his arms, in blessing the younger; and the Jews in their blindness make a cross of wood, that with it the blessing might be conferred on the Gentile.

S. Chrysostom says: Oh, high mystery, under the crossed arms of Jacob, Manasses lost his inheritance; so under the Cross of CHRIST Israel lost its pre-eminence, insomuch that as the Cross has conferred honour to the Church, it has covered the synagogue with infamy. The LORD did not give the Cross to Simon till He was without the gates of Jerusalem, and He did not confer His blessing on the Church till He was thrust out of the synagogue.

It is further to be noted that the cross made by Jacob was upon his breast, whilst that born by Christ and committed to Simon was laid on the back. This signifies that to the old Dispensation the cross was prospective, whilst to the Gentile Church it is retrospective. And, again, Israel made that sign as he was dying, on the day of his death; and the Jewish synagogue made the Cross for CHRIST on that day that its dispensation closed, and the life which had lingered in it, finally expired. By the Jews casting CHRIST forth, and by CHRIST giving His Cross to the Gentile, we may gather that our LORD never forgets us if we do not forget Him; nor forsakes us till we forsake Him; nor leaves us till we desert Him; nor estranges Himself from us till we utterly reject Him.

Remigius observes, The SON of GOD did not give His Cross to him who came out of Jerusalem, to go into the country, but to one coming out of the country towards Jerusalem. And S. Hilary says, that this is greatly to be wondered at. CHRIST chose to share in His sufferings one who was a stranger and a pagan, and disregarded those of His own nation; wherein He gave us to understand that He receives one sinner that repenteth rather than ninety and nine just persons that need no repentance. Or, as S. Jerome puts it more clearly, It is not to those who stray from the city of God that CHRIST commits His Cross, and unites to His sufferings, but to those who draw nigh to it. So He receives those who leave the world to approach Him, not those who fall from Him and turn to the world.

Thou dost love those, O Good JESUS, who love Thee, seeing that Thou didst meet Simon of Cyrene, and didst press forth without the city to receive him drawing nigh to Thee; so surely wilt Thou do to me if I seek Thee. Thou wilt meet me. Never dost Thou deny Thyself to him that asketh Thee, never hide Thyself from him that seeketh Thee.

Of Simon it is said that he was the father of Alexander and Rufus. To the Gentile Church CHRIST promises—"Instead of thy fathers, thou shalt have children whom thou mayest make princes in all lands;" and "Sing, O barren, thou that dost not bear; break forth into singing, and cry aloud, thou that didst not travail with child: for more are the children of the desolate than the children of the married wife, saith the LORD. . . . Thou shalt break forth on the right hand and on the left; and thy seed shall inherit the Gentiles, and make the desolate cities to be inhabited." Whilst to the Jewish Church, saith CHRIST, " Behold your house is left unto you desolate."

CHAPTER XIV.

On taking up one's Cross.

"IF any man will come after Me, let him deny himself, and take up his cross daily, and follow Me" (S. Luke ix. 23). This is as much as to say, If any man will keep My doctrine, and follow My steps, let him take up the cross, break his own will, and, treading in My footprints, he will reach Me.

S. Ambrose comments thus on this text: The Christian who will follow CHRIST must observe three conditions. The first is, that he bear the cross of his own free will, and not, like Simon, by constraint. For our LORD says, "If any man will," clearly showing that the cross-bearing must be voluntary. The SON of GOD would rather that we served Him not at all, than that we served Him by constraint, or for hire. CHRIST compels no man to serve Him, but leaves it to each man's free option to follow Him or not. In GOD'S house we are not slaves, but children.

The second condition is, that every man bear his own cross, and not, like Simon, that of another. "Let him take up *his* cross," are CHRIST'S words. Let no man then sustain his confidence in CHRIST'S merits alone, or in those of any Saint, without himself living a virtuous life, and bearing his own cross, and following CHRIST'S steps.

The third condition is, that a man bear the Cross for CHRIST'S sake, not out of hypocrisy, not to win the praise of men, but to bear the reproach of CHRIST.

That life which pious men lead, the sufferings they have to endure, the temptations with which they have to struggle—these all are crosses. So that life becomes a long journey of cross-bearing, a living martyrdom. S. Anselm in his Meditations says, When this name of the Cross sounds in thine ears, think not of the wooden tree, but of the cross of travail; for on the Cross of wood CHRIST hung but three hours, and on the cross of trouble He was stretched for thirty-three years.

CHRIST received of the Jews a cross of wood, dead and hard, but He has left us a living Cross in His Gospel, to which to conform our lives. He has not commanded us to die on a cross of wood, but to live by keeping the Gospel; thereby teaching us that He is better pleased for us to follow Him in His manner of living, than to imitate Him in that of dying. Whatever advantage there may be in the possession of a relic of the true Cross, that can only be the property of a few; but the life of CHRIST is for all, and in the keeping of CHRIST'S commandments is far higher advantage and greater profit every way. When the SON of GOD said, "The kingdom of Heaven suffereth violence, and the violent take it by storm," He admonished us that an evangelical life is nothing other than a rough and laborious cross, from which the worldling flies, but which the good embrace.

"If any man will follow Me, let him take up his cross." Not without a mystery did JESUS call His high doctrine and His precious life a cross, and call that cross man's, not His. That cross is ours. By the hands of the Cyrenian He conveyed and transmitted to us, on His way to Calvary, that most precious Cross of His.

O Good JESUS, Thou dost call the Cross, which is Thine, my cross! If the Cross be Thy doctrine, verily it is mine as well, for Thou givest it, and I keep it. If the Cross be one of wood on which Thou diest, then is that mine as well as Thine, for I live by Thy death thereon. If the Cross be suffering, then is it mine and Thine, for Thou didst suffer that I might follow Thy example.

After that CHRIST had committed His Cross to another, it made the Apostles and the glorious Martyrs cheerfully die for Him, knowing that by their agonies they were relieving His shoulder—filling up "that which is behind of the sufferings of CHRIST."

S. Cyril observes, that Those bear the cross with a willing mind, who endure what GOD calls them to suffer with a cheerful mind, for the love of CHRIST ; and these are rewarded not merely for the good works they do, but also for the spirit in which they are done. Those who bear the cross by constraint are those who do all that they are bound to do, murmuring and grudgingly ; the works of these are neither acceptable to GOD nor pleasing to man. Those who bear the cross for hire, are those who preach the Gospel for filthy lucre's sake. Oh, how many more disciples has Simon than CHRIST ! How many are there who, for a price, or by constraint, bear their Christianity, but who hate its yoke ! Those bear their cross by constraint who abstain from sin because they are not tempted ; or because they are afraid of losing position, or a good name, or character by indulging in that which is evil. And those bear it for hire who refrain from sin, and lead moral and Christian lives, that they may be well reported of men, and have the credit of sanctity. Some carry the Cross of CHRIST half the way only. These are they who begin with great fervour and devotion, but in time of temptation fall away or grow slack, and for earnestness assume indifference, from zealous become remiss. Some in childhood and youth bear the Cross of CHRIST with cheerfulness, eschewing the pomps and vanities of the world and the lusts of the flesh, and then, in the middle of their course, lay aside the Cross for ever. And others there are who, having spent their early life in sin, at middle age take up the Cross of CHRIST, and through the rest of life bear it lovingly.

Remigius observes, Seeing that the SON of GOD did not give up His Cross until He could bear it no longer, so ought we not to give up any Christian undertaking as long as the power remains to us to carry it out, however rough it may be to the shoulder, and however oppressive to the heart, till strength fails us. For our LORD will accept the bearing of the cross as far as we can, if only we carry it whither we ought.

When Lot was escaping from Sodom, the Angel bade him flee to the mountain ; but as Lot feared the mountain, he bade him rest in Zoar, half way. It is to be observed that the Angel commanded Lot in the first place to strive to reach the mountain ; by which we are taught that we are to aim at some higher pitch of excellence than we shall, in all pro-

On taking up one's Cross.

bability, arrive at. CHRIST, going to Calvary, left His Cross in the midst of His journey, as Lot, striving for the mountain, halted half way. We are given to understand by this how good our LORD is, how kind is the Master that we serve, for He is content in matters of His service if we begin well, and do the best we can, reckoning rather our purpose than our execution.

S. Gregory, in a pastoral, says, In the way of perfection, we will not say that he doth little who travails till he faint, and goeth onward till he falls. It is well for us to attempt in religion more than we think we can achieve, for often we are able to do far more than at first we supposed was possible. To this S. Anselm bears testimony. Of myself, he says, I say and confess that I am slothful. For I find that I can in many things advance if I have the courage to begin. And S. Bernard adds, At the very instant that the servant of our LORD determines with himself to serve GOD, immediately CHRIST is by to succour him. Of myself I dare affirm that I never encouraged a good thought without at once feeling CHRIST present at my side. Alas! how many there are who make the excuse of inability when a duty presents itself, who will not rise towards any height in religion because they will not venture to ascend. How many grovel on the plain, without so much as feeling an ambition to mount above it. What though they reach not the topmost pinnacle; is there not a Zoar half way, where they may be safe? What if the way to Calvary be long; can they not bear the cross till they sink?

Seneca remarks: I have seen many forbear from honest and virtuous lives, because they supposed themselves to be weak and tender. When they are asked how they know themselves not to be strong enough to make the attempt, they answer that they have never tried to live virtuous lives. In fact, they know vice by experience; they only guess at virtue.

It is to be observed that Simon took up the Cross late. Indeed, it is never too late to assume that cross. Judas took it up early, and laid it down soon. S. Paul caught it up late, and bore it to the end. Better is it to serve our Blessed LORD late, than to begin serving Him early, and then to give up His service at the best time of life.

In the parable, those were paid who went to labour in the

vineyard at the eleventh hour, the same as those who went early. Thereby our LORD shows Himself to be a just and merciful Judge, seeing that He paid the first who entered the vineyard what He had promised them, and gave the last more than they deserved. S. Gregory says in a homily, GOD, in rewarding and punishing, doth not tie Himself to the rigour of the law; for He punishes less than we deserve, and He pays more than we have a right to claim.

Learn then, O my Brother, that our LORD always gives good measure, pressed down and running over; and he that cometh to Him, however late, He will in no wise cast out. Late came the workmen into the vineyard, late to His disciples came CHRIST walking on the sea, late was the Cyrenian in shouldering the Cross, late was S. Paul in coming to the faith, late was the thief in crying out to his GOD. All these instances are given to comfort and encourage us; for by them we learn that late though it be that we enter into CHRIST'S service, He will not only receive us, but will give us a portion of His kingdom.

It was not without great mystery that CHRIST would not carry His Cross all the way, but that the Cyrenian should carry it for a part of the way, thus dividing the labour; for this was to give us to understand that we without Him cannot amend, nor will He pardon our sins without a movement on our parts. On His side there must be an advance towards us in mercy; on our side there must be a step towards Him in amendment.

The Cross Simon bore was one on which another was to suffer. There are many in this world who, Simon-like, are dragging about the crosses on which others are to writhe in agony. He carries a cross on which to crucify another, who with malicious and slanderous words injures the character of his neighbour. He, too, carries a cross whereon to crucify another, who exhorts another to the practice of piety, to self-denial, and to mortification, yet sets no good example in his own life. And those also prepare crosses for others, who lay on them burdens heavy to be borne, and yet do not touch them with so much as one of their fingers. Such is he who, without observing that which is most essential in the Christian religion, enforces the keeping of the ceremonial part.

CHAPTER XV.

The Weeping Women.

"THERE followed Him a great company of women, which also bewailed and lamented Him. But JESUS turning unto them said, Daughters of Jerusalem, weep not for Me, but weep for yourselves, and for your children" (S. Luke, xxiii. 27, 28). When CHRIST was being led to Calvary, a multitude of men and women accompanied Him, the men persecuting Him, the women bewailing Him. As He died for all, men and women, women as well as men were present at His death. Had He died among men only, some might have thought that redemption did not extend to women also. Therefore both were represented on Calvary.

One of the greatest mysteries to be noted in the Passion of the SON of GOD, is that the more He was tormented, the greater became His compassion, exhibited to these women, to His murderers, to the thief. Now, the SON of GOD, moving barefoot towards Calvary, despised, rejected, bruised, bleeding, faint, and weary, turns His head, and comforts the women that follow Him weeping. He did not raise His eyes to Pilate, nor open His mouth to Herod; yet how readily He turns His face to the daughters of Zion, and comforts them with holy words. The king and the governor had conjured Him to speak, and He answered them not; women weep, and He turns to console them.

Had not the tears of these poor women streamed over their cheeks, He would not have spoken to them; but the face of JESUS looked on them because their own faces were bathed in tears.

O my soul, behold how the daughters of Zion and the afflicted JESUS are drawn to each other; wherefore shouldst thou not be among them and hear His words and receive His look? When He looked on S. Peter, that look broke up the fountain of the Apostle's tears, and now the tears of the women attract the look of CHRIST. CHRIST going to Calvary is like a general with His army, says Remigius; He heads the host and He turns to encourage the laggards. What other meaning has this act of JESUS in turning to talk with women, whilst at another time He is in company with men, but that He is not careless of the perfect who go before, nor forgetful of the feeble who stay behind. What comfort it is to sinful souls to know that CHRIST should turn to speak to these poor women, for thereby they are given hope and confidence that He will not withdraw His eyes from those who serve Him imperfectly, nor hide His face from those who follow at a distance. That which CHRIST did was out of pure mercy, without having been requested by the women, or ordered by the executioner.

Let it also be noted that the tears drew CHRIST to turn and look upon the mourners. And it is chiefly in times of sorrow, above all, in seasons of grief for sin, that He lifts up the light of His countenance upon us, to turn our heaviness into joy, and to wipe the tears from the eyes.

O my soul, follow in the train of these holy women of Jerusalem, and weep with them, for then will the SON of GOD turn and look upon thee.

S. Bonaventura says, O Good JESUS, Redeemer of my soul, in the midst of Thy anguish Thou didst feel for these daughters of Zion! Wondrous mystery is it, that on the journey to Calvary JESUS is related to have spoken only to these sorrowing women. For our LORD highly regards those who follow Him in His Passion, suffering with Him, that they may be glorified together.

Whither shall the SAVIOUR turn His eyes? If He look down, He sees the dirt that is cast at Him; if He looks up, He sees Calvary whereon He is to die; if He looks on one side, behold the thieves who are to suffer with Him; if He looks on the other, He sees the executioner who is to fasten Him to the

Cross; if He looks before, behold an infuriate rabble; but if He looks behind, He discerns weeping women.

JESUS, knowing that His life drew to an end, though His office of mercy was not limited, turned His face to the daughters of Jerusalem, and with His eyes fixed on them, spake to them tenderly, bidding them refrain from weeping for Him, but urging them to shed tears for themselves and for their children. By which He meant this—Weep not for One Who is innocent, but lament for the guilty; weep not for Him Who sheds His Blood, but for those on whom that Blood descends in doom. Thus, we should not weep for the death of Abel, but for the malice of Cain; nor for the captivity of Joseph, but for the envy of his brethren; nor for the persecution of David, but for the jealousy of Saul; nor for the banishment of Elijah, but for the wickedness of Jezebel; nor for the martyrdom of Isaiah, but for the cruelty of Manasses. "Weep not for the dead, neither bemoan him: but weep sore for him that goeth away; for he shall return no more, nor see his native country" (Jer. xxii. 10).

S. Maximus, in one of his sermons on the Saints, says, When you hear of a great martyrdom, and of the sufferings of the Martyrs, you should envy them; but on the tyrants who tortured them have great pity, for the torments of the Saints ended in an hour, whilst those of their persecutors last to this day. And Origen pertinently observes, that There is enough reason for us to weep for ourselves, without sighing over the death of CHRIST; for He had rather see hearts broken and contrite for sin, than mere mourning, without penitence, over His Passion.

S. Augustine says, The SON of GOD by these words, "Weep not for Me," releases thee from lamenting for Him; and by the words, "but weep for yourselves," imposes on us the obligation to bewail our transgressions. And S. Basil beautifully adds, Seeing CHRIST said to the daughters of Jerusalem who followed Him, "Weep not for Me, but weep for yourselves," my Brother, you ought to give over weeping, and to begin to amend; for GOD had rather see thee give no cause to weep, than weep incessantly for repeated falls. On the words of the Apocalypse, "GOD shall wipe away all tears from their eyes;" the Venerable Bede writes, What else is it for GOD to dry the tears, than to give grace no more to sin. For till man sinned, he knew not how to weep; and when in Heaven his tears are dried, it will be because sin is no more.

S. Jerome says, in a letter to Priscilla, that it is better to weep for those who live in sin than for those who die in sanctity. The good who die enter into rest, but the wicked who live accumulate guilt for their damnation. Weep not then, says CHRIST, O daughters of Jerusalem, for My death, which is so glorious, but weep for the lives of yourselves and your children, which are so evil; "If they have done these things in a green tree, what shall be done in a dry?" If they have cut Me off and rent Me, Who am a green Tree Whose leaf shall not wither, and which is for the healing of the nations, what will become of the dry, unprofitable tree of the Jewish stock? It will be cut down, for it cumbereth the ground.

CHAPTER XVI.

Jesus stripped of His Garments.

"AND they crucified Him, and parted His garments" when they had brought Him to Calvary, says S. Matthew (xxvii. 35).

That is to say, the SON of GOD reached the top of Calvary, wearied and faint, as also did Simon the Cyrenian, laden with the Cross. Then the executioners busied themselves to take from CHRIST His apparel, without giving Him time to rest. These garments were necessarily taken from Him before they nailed Him to the Cross.

S. Chrysostom says, Because the torments had been so many and the way so long, and the Mount Calvary somewhat high, the Blessed JESUS came to it wearied and full of anguish, so that He could not bare Himself of His clothes, but suffered His tormentors to strip Him of His raiment.

What meaneth this, O Good JESUS? Doth it not suffice that on the Cross Thine executioners take away Thy life, but must they rob Thee of Thy raiment also? How bountiful Thou art, O my SAVIOUR! To S. John Thou confidest Thy Mother, to the FATHER Thou committest Thy soul, to Nicodemus Thou entrustest Thy Body, to the world Thou surrenderest Thy Blood, to the thief Thou givest Paradise, to the soldiers Thou yieldest Thy garments. GOD bade Moses take a burnt sacrifice of the herd, a male without blemish, and flay it, and sprinkle the blood round about the altar, and lay the wood in order, and the sacrifice upon it (Lev. i.). This was typical of CHRIST the true Sacrifice, Who was without spot, Who had sprinkled the ground about the Altar of His Cross with His Blood, Who was now to be stretched on that wood laid in order, and Who was now stripped of His covering. The Psalmist, speaking in the Name of CHRIST, as the executioners unrobe Him, says, "Shame hath covered My face." Which is as though He said, Among all the great and cruel torments that I have endured, the greatest is this, seeing Myself exposed before the eyes of My enemies, and My garments taken off from Me one by one.

The SON of GOD, full of modesty and shamefacedness, now beholds Himself on the top of the hill, unclothed, among that multitude of gazers. No man, says S. Augustine, is so poor but he has a garment to die in and a sheet to be buried in, unless it be the Holy JESUS, to Whom they have not left so much as a coat to be executed in, or a shroud in which to be entombed.

"They stript Joseph out of his coat; and they took him, and cast him into a pit, and the pit was empty, there was no water in it" (Gen. xxxvii. 23, 24). That is, when Joseph had come to his envious brethren at a convenient time for them to execute their malicious purpose against him, they took off him the garment of colours that he wore, and cast him into an empty well. Joseph was the best-beloved son of his father Jacob, and was hated accordingly of his brethren. Joseph was a type of CHRIST. When the FATHER said on Tabor, "This is My Beloved SON," did He not plainly tell us that this was the SON in Whom he was well pleased, and did most rejoice? And CHRIST was hated of His brethren for reproving their vices, and for the miracles He wrought. As Joseph was stripped of his coat, so was CHRIST of His seamless robe; and as Joseph was cast into the dry pit, so was JESUS given over to a death of parching thirst, without water to slake the burning tongue. Oh, how far more terrible was Calvary than Sychem! Joseph went up from his well alive, but CHRIST descended from His Cross dead. From Joseph the brethren took only his garment, but JESUS was robbed of His garments and His life.

For the SON of GOD to despoil Himself of His garments before ascending the Cross, is to teach us that if we would mount to any height of perfection, we must divest ourselves of our wills, our worldly desires, our covetousness. CHRIST first surrendered His will in the garden when He said, "Not as I will, but as Thou wilt," and now He perfects that oblation by yielding up His garments. If we would be like Him we must strip our hearts of their carnal appetites, of which the clothing is a figure.

Saul "stripped off his clothes also, and prophesied before Samuel in like manner" (1 Sam. xix. 24). That is to say, as soon as King Saul divested himself of his royal robes, the Spirit of Prophecy descended upon him; but as soon as he vested himself again in his princely attire, that Spirit deserted him. S. Isidore, on these words remarks, King Saul was only received into the choir of Prophets when he had doffed his royal robes; this is to teach us, that if we will be of the number of the elect, we must despoil ourselves of our vain desires, our worldly pomp, and self-will. Agmon notes that at the instant that Saul resumed his garments the Prophetic Spirit left him, from which we may infer that how much the less is our part in the world, so much the higher it is in CHRIST, and that the greater it is in the world, the less it is in CHRIST. In princely robes, Saul was an earthly king; stripped of them, he was an inspired Prophet. "He that humbleth himself shall be exalted."

Saul did well to unvest, but erred in clothing himself again. It is better to be stripped of worldly favours and be in favour with GOD, than to be enveloped in the world's pomp and to be found naked before GOD. "I counsel thee to buy of Me white raiment, that thou mayest be clothed, and that the shame of thy nakedness do not appear. Because thou sayest, I am rich, and increased with goods, and have need of nothing; and knowest not that thou art wretched, and miserable, and poor, and blind, and naked."

O my soul, art not thou ashamed to go clothed in thy self-will when thy Master is stripped? Dost thou boast thyself in thy garments, which are but filthy rags? Strip them off, that with them the Good JESUS may be clothed withal; for those sins which invest thee must be placed on Him, that He may nail them in His own body to the Tree. My soul, when thou thinkest thyself to be clothed, then art thou naked, and poor, and miserable before GOD; but when thou divestest thyself of self of bad habits, of pride, of covetousness, then art thou clothed in the marriage garment by Him.

CHRIST, "His own self, bore our sins in His own body on the tree" (1 Pet. ii. 24). Stripping Himself of His Majesty, He clothed Himself in our sins, and bare them on the Cross of shame. Then, says S. John Damascene, did He bear our sins in His own body on the tree, when the Eternal FATHER beheld His Dear SON'S members draped in our sins, when CHRIST and they, and they with CHRIST, were executed on the Cross.

CHAPTER XVII.

The Third Hour.

"AND it was the third hour, and they crucified Him," says S. Mark (xv. 25). Having unbound His hands, removed the rope from His neck, stripped Him of His raiment, the murderers place Him on the Cross between two thieves, as though he had been their captain.

For such high mysteries as are here to be considered, it would require the tongue of Angels, the spirit of Prophets, the gifts of Apostles, the contemplation of Religious, to consider them aright; for the mysteries of the Cross and the sorrows of the Passion of CHRIST, are better tasted than described. I call upon Thee then, O wounded CHRIST, and beseech Thee that Thou wilt guide my pen in what I write; and soften my heart, that writing I may feel; and dissolve my eyes, that feeling I may weep. O Good JESUS, O Love of my soul, if I could feel some portion, however small, of what Thou endurest, and could taste a little of that bitterness which Thou quaffest, how were it possible for my hand to write, or my eyes to refrain from tears?

"She weepeth sore in the night, and her tears are on her cheeks," says the Prophet (Lam. i. 2), speaking of sorrowful Jerusalem, with her walls beaten down and her children in captivity. How much greater occasion is there now for the tears of Zion to flow; after that desolation there was restoration, after this there is none. Jeremiah wept for the captivity of the Jewish nation, for the breaking down of the walls of the city; and shall not tears flow for the slaying of the SON of GOD and the rending of His sacred limbs? Comfortless Jeremiah cannot console himself when he sees the streets of Salem grown with grass; and can tears be restrained when they lie sprinkled with the Redeemer's Blood? Lend me, O great Prophet, some of thy tears, that I may weep, not for the stones of the Holy City, which are to be overthrown, but for the sins of my soul; for though it be true that the Jews crucified the LORD of Glory, yet I know full well that the cause of that Crucifixion was my sin.

It is time now that we speak of the great and marvellous spectacle offered to the world at this moment. S. Bernard says, We shall highly esteem this spectacle of CHRIST on Calvary offering Himself to death, because He offered Himself willingly, the love in His heart being of such fervency that it overmastered the pain He endured in His Soul and body.

GOD " brought me into the land of Israel, and set me upon a very high mountain—and, behold, there was a Man, whose appearance was like the appearance of brass, with a line of flax in his hand, and a measuring reed " (Ezek. xl. 2, 3). That is to say, Among the great visions I, Ezekiel, saw on the river Cobar, was one in which I was placed on a mountain near Jerusalem, where I saw a Man standing alone, with a reed six cubits in length, with which he measured the new building which was being erected in that place.

Such, without all doubt, was a wonderful figure; but yet the fulfilling of it is more wonderful still, seeing that in it are symbolized various mysteries concerning the death of CHRIST.

This new building signifies the blessed Humanity of CHRIST, newer than all the novelties of the world, for He alone was Virgin-born, conceived by the HOLY GHOST, free from all spot of sin. The high mountain seen by the Prophet is Calvary, on which CHRIST suffered; it is called high, not on account of its great altitude, but on account of the loftiness of the mysteries it was found worthy to have enacted on it, and of the elevation in dignity it achieved by having been sprinkled with the SAVIOUR'S own most precious Blood.

The reed with which the new building is measured is the Cross of Shame; and he who measures the building with the reed is the Jewish people, engaged in stretching the sacred members of CHRIST upon it; measuring His Divine Person lengthways from His sacred head to His feet, and in breadth from one extended and Almighty hand to the other.

And what was signified by the six cubits, but that this act was to be consummated in the sixth age of the world, and at the sixth hour. Six in Holy Scripture is the number of sin. Six lambs were offered as a sin-offering on the day of the new moon; the image of gold set up in the plains of Dura was six cubits in breadth; the height of Goliath, who defied GOD'S people, was six cubits and a span; there are six things that the LORD hateth, saith Solomon; six years had Jacob to serve for the cattle; six were the troubles of Job; six years had the bondman to be subject to his master before his release; and the number of multiplied transgressions summed up in Antichrist is six hundred and sixty and six.

It is to be observed that Jerusalem was measured with this six-cubit reed in the vision of Ezekiel; that is, with the Cross. With the measure the Jews applied to CHRIST, by that same measure shall they be tried, "With what measure ye mete, it shall be measured to you again." It is also to be noted that the Man did not measure the length, but the breadth of the temple; that is, the Jews with their cross tried the body of CHRIST, but could not prove His Divinity, which can neither be weighed nor measured, for GOD is without limit and without end.

It is further to be observed that the reed was touched by the Man with one hand only, wherein is signified that, although the Jew measured the SON of GOD with the reed of punishment, yet he touched Him not with the rod of sin, for none could stain or spot the innocency and purity of CHRIST.

The hour being come in which the true Isaac was to be sacrificed, He was commanded by the executioners to extend Himself on the Cross, that they might see where the holes were to be bored into which the nails were to be driven. S. Anselm says, That to put a man on a cross, and there to crucify Him with nails, is the most terrible and most humiliating of deaths. Yet terrible and shameful though it were, CHRIST needed no second command to make Him lie down on the wood and measure Himself on the Tree; for during thirty and three years His grief had ever been before Him, and He had been betrothed to the Cross. Sorrowful, JESUS at the third hour was laid, stripped of His garments, on the Cross to be measured for the holes; then removed, that the holes might be bored. The Cross lying on the ground, CHRIST stretched Himself at length upon it, and was measured, but measured with so little care, that the executioners made the holes somewhat further apart than they should have made them. And this is what is meant by the words, "All My bones are out of joint," namely, that when CHRIST was nailed to the Cross, His sacred members had to be forced and strained until the hands could reach the holes which had been made in haste and carelessness by the executioners.

O my soul, how is it possible that thou art not dismayed, seeing thy LORD in such a strait? How should not the heavens tremble and hell quake, seeing JESUS measured "Who hath measured the waters in the hollow of His hand, and meted out heaven with the span, and comprehended the dust of the earth in a measure, and weighed the mountains in scales, and the hills in a balance?" (Isa. xl. 12.)

O Good JESUS, Redeemer of my soul, by this mystery I conjure Thee, and for the reverence of this spectacle I beseech Thee, that when, before Thy tribunal, my merits shall be measured with my demerits, Thou wilt have more pity on me than the tormentors had on Thee. For if Thou measurest according to Thy justice, and not according to Thy mercy, I know that I shall be found wanting.

S. Bernard remarks that there was something to be done by all who were collected on the top of Mount Calvary. Some of the tormentors bored the holes for the nails, whilst others sorted the nails, the centurion guarded CHRIST, the Jews mocked, the soldiers took charge of the raiment, Magdalene sighed, Blessed Mary wept, John gazed aghast, Angels wondered, and the very elements were troubled.

The Cross having been prepared, the nails having been selected, the executioners again placed our LORD upon the Tree. They had been paid by the Jews, who would not themselves take part in the Crucifixion, lest they, forsooth, should be defiled. And now the hour had come for the sacred Humanity to be martyred, and the Redemption of mankind to be perfected. Stretch Thyself at length then! O Good JESUS, cast Thyself, O my Redeemer, on this Thy last bed; lie Thee down for the last time, but not in peace to take Thy rest, but in the battle to be racked with pain; not for sweet and balmy sleep, but for a bitter and torturing death. "They pierced My hands and My feet, I may tell all My bones," saith the Psalmist, speaking in the Person of CHRIST, as if he would say: At the sixth hour they nailed Me to the Cross, piercing My hands with rough large nails, and bruising and transfixing My feet, and so ruthlessly disjointing My bones and straining My sinews, that no member of My body was without pain, no bone was unreckoned. S. Augustine says on these words, That as David had prophesied, so was it fulfilled; for on the cursed Tree CHRIST'S hands were pierced with nails, and all His bones were wrenched asunder.

At the time that the nail entered the hand of CHRIST—and we believe that the left hand was the first that was transfixed—the flesh was broken, the skin was torn, the sinews shrank, the bones were out of joint, and the heart in the midst of the body was even as melting wax.

With wonderful beauty does S. Cyril remark that, Now was CHRIST suffering in His hand for the sin of the hand of Adam. For as Adam stretched forth his hand to take the fruit, so now does the Second Adam stretch forth His hand to gather of the result of that fruit-eating—Death. Many thousand years had passed since that sin had been committed; and now the penalty is paid. The heart of Adam lusted after the fruit, his hand took, his lips tasted; and now the Second Adam's heart is pierced, His hand is transfixed, and His lips are parched, in making amends for the transgression of the first Adam.

CHAPTER XVIII.

The Nailing of the Hands.

"HOW is the hammer of the whole earth cut asunder and broken!" exclaims the Prophet Jeremiah (l. 23). That is to say, Rejoice, O house of Israel; be glad, O inhabitants of Zion, for the hammer that smote the whole earth, and filled it with the sound of its blows, is cut asunder and broken to pieces.

This was said, in the first place, of Babylon, which oppressed Israel, whose power was shattered, so that it could oppress the elect people no more. But it has a further and a deeper signification. It refers mainly to Satan, who is indeed the hammer of the whole earth, smiting, bruising, crushing, grinding to powder. The hammer is Satan, says Origen, nailing the wicked to the torturing rack of the world with the iron of vices. For the Devil has his crucifixions as well as CHRIST. Satan racks his servants a little now, and very much hereafter; whilst CHRIST gives them crosses here, but crowns hereafter. With three nails only was the SON of GOD nailed to the tree, but Satan fastens his victims to their cross of anguish with a thousand vices, which he smites and rivets with the hammer of temptation. When David fell, was he not smitten by the hammer of the whole world? When Solomon left the worship of GOD for the idolatries of his wives, had not the hammer fallen on his wisdom? Was it not the hammer of the whole earth that clenched the chains and smote out the eyes of Manasses? And now that hammer descends with all its force on CHRIST, and in nailing Him to the Cross, is itself cut asunder and broken.

For the words of the Prophet signify this, that by the Passion of CHRIST the power of the Devil was broken, for the SON of GOD suffered Himself to be fastened to the Cross for this cause, that the great Enemy of souls might, in that final act of malice, exhaust his powers. Now the Serpent bruises the heel of the Seed of the Woman, whilst that Seed crushes the Serpent's head. Temptation may assail us, but it cannot break us, without our free-will and consent. The hammer may smite, but it cannot hurt, unless we permit it. Temptation has lost its power, in that CHRIST with every temptation makes a way to escape, or gives ample power to resist; so that now it is no more to be feared. Indeed, now the endurance of temptation is profitable and meritorious. "Blessed is the man that endureth temptation: for when he is tried, he shall receive the crown of life" (S. James i. 12). And thus the heaviest blow of the broken hammer may advance greatly our position in the kingdom of the Resurrection; and, far from crushing and breaking, it may mould us into perfection.

On this S. Gregory beautifully says, CHRIST has left the Devil and his hammer broken and bruised; or if He has left him any strength at all, it is not to tempt, so much as to exercise us; insomuch that the trials of this world are but the vegetation of the field, from which indeed the spider may gather poison, but from which also the bee may draw honey.

The left hand of JESUS having been nailed, the torturers sought to nail also the right hand. And some interpreters of the passage, "All My bones are out of joint," have supposed that the sinews of our Blessed LORD had so contracted with a spasm of pain, through the nailing of the left hand, that by this means the right hand did not reach the hole which had been bored to receive the nail that was to transfix it; and this necessitated the rending and straining of the nerves, and the disjointing of the bones to which the Psalmist alludes. O Virgin Mother, dost thou hear the sound of the joints, and the cracking of the sinews, as they are drawn out for the nailing of the right hand? Surely the hammer that smites in the nails is also a sword which pierces through the Mother's soul. At one and the same time the hammer drives the cruel iron through the palms of the

SON, and smites into the heart of the Mother. She is martyred in her eyes, in seeing so many wounds; in her ears, in hearing so many blasphemies; in her body, through great grief and anguish; and in her heart, by feeling that her Divine SON is dying.

"There was neither hammer nor axe nor any tool of iron heard in the house, while it was in building" (1 Kings vi. 7), is said of Solomon's temple; for the boards were carefully made to join, and the timber so accurately measured, that when the wood was brought to be put together, no axe-blow was given, nor was sound of hammer heard. It is also written in the first Book of Samuel (xiii. 19), "There was no smith found throughout all the land of Israel;" for the Philistines had forbidden the Hebrews to have a forge or smith throughout the land, lest they should make weapons.

O glorious law! Would that it had lasted to the coming of CHRIST; for, if there had been no smith in Jerusalem, they could not have crucified the SON of GOD with nails. To build the temple of Solomon there were no nails used, no stroke of hammer was heard; but in the Sacred Temple that the HOLY GHOST framed, the hammer resounds on the nails, yet not at its construction, but at its undoing. As with Solomon's temple, so with the Temple of the HOLY GHOST. In silence and in quietness was that Temple of GOD among men reared, in the stillness of the Virgin's Womb was It fitted and framed; but in Its dissolution hammer and nails were used. And thus it was of old with the glorious temple of Solomon, that was built noiselessly, but the King of Babylon "set fire upon the holy places" and "broke down all the carved work thereof with axes and hammers."

O princes of the Philistines, why do ye suffer the Jews to have a forge on Mount Calvary, and there to use the hammer with such deadly effect, so that the sound is heard in Earth, in Heaven, and in Hell? In Earth is heard that hammer nailing the sins of that earth to the tree; in Heaven is heard the hammer of Jael smiting the nail into the head of Sisera; in Hell is heard that hammer forging the great chain, and fashioning the key that shall bind and lock up that old Serpent, which is the Devil.

O cruel nails! O ruthless hammer! Seeing ye do not touch

The Nailing of the Hands.

the planed boards in Solomon's temple, why do ye now break these holy hands? What news is this, O Israel? Was there not, until this time, a smith to be found in the kingdom to sharpen the coulters, the axes, and the mattocks; and now there is no lack of a smith to make and strike the nails into the hands and feet of the SON of the Most High?

Awake, O my soul, at the sound of the hammer, and bid it break the rock of thy hard and impenitent heart in pieces! (Isa. xxiii. 29). Who but I have forged these nails, which transfix my GOD? For are not they my mortal offences which are as of iron that enter into His soul, and nail Him to the tree?

CHAPTER XIX.

The Lifting of the Cross.

"AND the LORD spake unto Moses, saying, Speak unto the children of Israel, and say unto them, When ye be come into the land which I give unto you, and shall reap the harvest thereof, then ye shall bring a sheaf of the first fruits of your harvest unto the priest : and he shall wave the sheaf before the LORD, to be accepted for you" (Lev. xxiii. 9—11). We shall not be far wrong if we say that the Land of Promise is the Catholic Church, the seed sown are the Faithful, the reaping is death, and the first fruit of that harvest is CHRIST, Who was taken and lifted up as a wave offering.

We may observe that GOD did not order a great deal to be offered to Him, but merely one sheaf; to teach us thereby, that it was not the greatness of His Divinity, but the lowliness of His Humanity which was offered before the FATHER. S. Cyril comments thus on the passage : Note and mark well, that of all the shocks, GOD only required one to be presented to Him ; because of all the men that ever have been born into the world, or ever shall be born, CHRIST alone was the One, All-prevailing, Only Sacrifice to be accepted of GOD ; and that all the other sheaves are accepted, and blessed, and ransomed through the Oblation of this One Sheaf.

S. Matthew, in his genealogy of CHRIST, recites fourteen princes, fourteen nobles, and fourteen priests, all which catalogue he brings to prove that, of all these two and forty sheaves, the One Sheaf of CHRIST alone was that which was accepted as the wave offering to GOD.

Origen considers that the shock of many ears bound up symbolized the union which the WORD made with man, the which was faithfully and surely bound and knit together; and though at His Passion it was slackened, yet it was never dissolved. Neither was it without mystery that GOD commanded that this sheaf should be exalted to the highest place in the temple; for this prefigured the elevation of CHRIST to be looked upon by those who pierced Him, and to be worshipped by those who loved Him.

It is to be observed that the priest, in the oblation of the sheaf, elevated and then waved it, thereby making the sign of the Holy Cross, and foreshadowing the crucifixion of " CHRIST the First Fruits " of the quick and dead.

Returning now to Calvary, we see the uplifting of the Cross between Heaven and Earth, reconciling both. It is traditionally held that, on the raising of the Cross, the hands of CHRIST were nailed, but not His sacred feet; and this is probable, for the executioner could hardly have judged where to nail the feet till the body of our Divine LORD was actually suspended: and indeed it is somewhat difficult to suppose that the feet could have been nailed before the Cross was uplifted. As the Cross was lifted and cast into the hole which had been made to receive it, the body of CHRIST quivered at the stroke, causing fresh pain; for it strained open the wounds in His hands, allowing the blood to well forth.

S. Anselm, in his " Meditations," says, When the tormentors elevated the Cross, with CHRIST suspended on it, the thorns were moved from their places; the wounds gaped; the nails bent under the weight; the flesh where it had cleaved separated; and streams of blood gushed from His temples, from His back, and from His hands, flowing over His shoulders and breast, and bathing Him from head to foot.

At the lifting up of the Cross, says Ubertinus, the tormentors shouted, the Pharisees and Scribes cried out triumphantly, His friends wept, His acquaintance grieved, and strangers compassionated Him. Observe how the same event may influence in a different way different people. A piteous sight such as this melts the merciful hearts, and hardens the pitiless.

"He hath no form nor comeliness; and when we shall see Him there is no beauty that we should desire Him" (Is. liii. 2). That is, the SON of GOD was such upon the Cross that those who knew Him could hardly recognise Him. His flesh was bruised, His skin mangled, His bones out of joint, His face sullied with spitting, His hair plucked off and draggled with blood, His eyes dim. This text of Isaiah needs no explanation, says S. Jerome, for it is to be taken literally, as applying to our Blessed LORD.

Remigius puts the matter thus, with no little beauty and feeling: CHRIST despoiled Himself of His garments to clothe us, of His merits to invest us, of His honour to ennoble us, of His life to vivify us, of His comeliness to beautify us. Had He not given us His merits at the foot of the Cross, what would have become of us? Who would have tasted of Eternal Life, had not CHRIST yielded us His life? How could we have appeared before His holy face, had not our LORD adorned us with His beauty? How is it possible, O Isaiah, that the SON of GOD should not seem uncomely to thee, seeing that upon His shoulders are laid all the pollutions of the world? And Agmon says, Not without mystery does Isaiah say that there is no form, nor beauty, nor comeliness in CHRIST, and also that there is no token that there has been any in Him; for all that could profit us He gave us, and all that could injure or prejudice us, He took upon Himself.

The executioner, perceiving that the bleeding body of the SAVIOUR hung by the hands alone, now nailed the feet; not meaning thereby to mitigate His sufferings, but to expedite His death. Taking a nail in one hand, he put one foot over the other on the Cross—the left foot upon the right, it is believed—and smote; and the iron passed through the quivering nerves, severing the delicate veins, going between the slender bones, boring through both feet, and so, through into the wood.

S. Bernard, in his "De Planctu Virginis," writes, O comfortless Mother! tell me, I beseech thee, those continual blows, that playing of the arms, that jerking breath of him who smites, where did they cause anguish, save in thy sorrowful heart? O cruel enemies! doth not the law, in which ye make your boast, forbid

you to seethe the kid in its mother's milk, and to kill at once
the ewe with its lamb? What! are you not breaking the law in
torturing the SON in the sight of the Mother who bare Him,
and at whose breasts He sucked?

At the stroke of the hammer, the whole Cross shivered, and
the wounds of Him Who hung upon it gaped and distilled blood.
Streams bubbled out of the palms, and two fountains burst forth
from the feet.

O most bountiful Redeemer! since one drop of Thy Blood
would suffice to redeem the world, why dost Thou shed all that
Thy veins can yield? Oh, how well does the Prophet say, "With
the LORD there is mercy; and with Him is plenteous redemption" (Ps. cxxx. 7), for that on the Altar of the Cross this day,
there abound oblations, griefs, sacrifices, love. There is no stint,
no short measure. Verily, "where sin abounded, Grace did much
more abound" (Rom. v. 21).

Comfortless Mother of my GOD! although the Sacrifice which
is offered this day on Calvary be grievous to thee, and cost thy
SON dear, yet it is accepted by the Eternal FATHER, and it
is a satisfaction for the sins of the whole world.

CHAPTER XX.

The Lots cast.

"AND they crucified Him, and parted His garments, casting lots: that it might be fulfilled which was spoken by the Prophet, They parted My garments among them, and upon My vesture did they cast lots" (S. Matt. xxvii. 35). When the torturers had left CHRIST crucified, they agreed to divide the prey between them; and this consisted in a loose upper garment, and the seamless robe, which S. Augustine thinks was knit like a glove.

The Venerable Bede writes thus on S. Luke, CHRIST showed Himself to be very holy everywhere, but chiefly on Calvary, for there He exhibited His great charity, in offering up Himself to die; His great patience, in enduring such great pains; His great abstinence, in tasting only of vinegar and gall; His great humility, in dying between two thieves; His great clemency, in praying for His murderers; and His great poverty, in leaving behind Him only His garments.

S. Hilary says, The SON of GOD commended poverty to us rather by example than by word of mouth, seeing that on His death-day He left no kingdom to be divided, no heirs to whom His inheritance might fall, no money to bestow, no jewels to distribute, no houses to bequeath. For what treasure could He have hoarded up, Who was indebted to another for His shroud and for His grave? He was born in a stable, and He died on a charnel-heap. He entered the world in the midst of cattle; He left it among thieves. Living, He had not where to lay His head; and in dying He had no place in which to repose His body.

O Good JESUS, exclaims S. Bernard, how dare I accumulate earthly possessions and costly raiment, when I raise my eyes to Thee on the Cross and see Thee deprived of all! Naked came our Blessed LORD from His Mother's womb into this world, and in nakedness does He leave it.

"They part My garments among them: and cast lots for My vesture," says David, in the Person of CHRIST. How is this, that mention is made of the vesture and the garments being divided, and none of the severing of the joints and parting of the bones? How is this, that in death He takes account of what becomes of His raiment, which at best was but the clothing of a poor Man? Dost Thou speak of Thy coat severed, and make no mention of Thy thorn-rent head? Surely the allusion to the parted garments and allotted vesture draws our attention to them as involving some great mystery.

The garments were divided into four parts, to every soldier a part; but for our LORD'S seamless robe they cast lots whose it should be.

What is signified by the vesture of CHRIST, but the Catholic Faith, one and undivided, like the seamless robe, and yet parted to the four quarters of the earth, like the divided garments?

Four were the limbs of the Cross, from four wells pour forth four streams of Blood, and into four portions the garments are parted. For through the length and breadth of earth, north and south, and east and west, the Cross stretches, extending redemption, and the Blood streams, bearing life to Angels in heaven, to the departed in waiting expectation for the Blood of the Covenant, which should send forth the prisoners out of the pit (Zech. ix. 11), to the wicked for pardon, to the elect to unite to Him.

"A river went out of Eden to water the garden; and thence it was parted, and became into four heads" (Gen. ii. 10). Now from the heart of JESUS flows the river of Blood, parting into four streams, and issuing from His hands and His feet. "And the name of the first is Pison: that is it which compasseth the whole land of Havilah, where there is gold; and the gold of that land is good: there is bdellium and the onyx stone." Is not this the stream that enters Heaven, and compasses the City of GOD, a land where gold is good, where treasures are opened to man by that river. And Gihon "is it that compasseth the whole land of Ethiopia," bearing life and light to them that sit in darkness and in the shadow of death. And to the banished in Assyria flows Hiddekel, bringing restoration. And Euphrates, which is by interpretation, "that which maketh fruitful," is the stream by which are planted the elect, bringing forth their fruit in due season.

But to speak of the garments. S. Hilary says, That the vesture of the SON of GOD not being divided among those who stood afar off weeping, but among those who slew CHRIST, was for this, that our Redeemer came to call sinners to repentance, not just persons who needed no repentance—that He came to the sick, not to the whole.

O depth of the Charity of CHRIST! He dispossessed Himself of all, that I might inherit; He gave His garments to me, that I might not be found naked, but that I might "be clothed upon, that mortality might be swallowed up of life."

The garments were divided, to show the extent to which the Church should spread, namely to each quarter of the heavens; but the one robe was not rent, to show that the Church, though scattered throughout the world, was yet One. So are there many seas lapping many lands, but one surrounding ocean.

S. Hilary observes that the SON of GOD must have had some mystery involved in His garments, otherwise Holy Scripture would not make such account of them—David prophesying of them, CHRIST fulfilling the prophecy, the Evangelists recording what was done.

There is another interpretation given by ancient writers of the garments. They say that that which was divided into four parts represented CHRIST'S human body, which was rent by His enemies, whilst the seamless robe symbolized His mystical body, the Church, which they could not rend; or had not then the opportunity of rending, but which would be torn by heretics, as His human body was lacerated by Jews and Gentiles. S. Augustine, commenting on S. John, says, That by the common garment which the SON of GOD suffered to be divided, is understood His precious body, which He gave to be broken and rent, and by the coat without seam, which He would not suffer them to tear, is signified the holy Church, which no man shall dissolve; for "he that toucheth you, toucheth the apple of His eye," saith Zechariah (ii. 8); that is, GOD will not suffer any to offend His members in the Church. And it may very clearly be seen (says S. Cyril) how much more CHRIST loves His Church than His own body, for He gave His body to be mangled, but He will not endure that His Church be touched.

S. Basil, on the text in the Psalm observes, The good Christian ought to have great regard to that which he does, and the heretic should consider well what he is about; for CHRIST more easily pardons them who divide the garment of His flesh than those who rend the unity of the Church. And S. Jerome says, The heretics who cause schism in CHRIST'S Church are worse than the executioners who laid hands on CHRIST, for they spared the seamless coat of the Faith, which heretics lightly undertake to rend asunder.

CHAPTER XXI.

The Seamless Robe.

"NOW the coat was without seam, woven from the top throughout," says S. John (xix. 24).

The SON of GOD left us the seamless robe, which is His Church, entire and unrent, clean, and woven from the top, that is, from Him Who is its Head, and throughout perfectly united together in texture, the parts to one another, and all to the top whence the weaving began. CHRIST gave His Name to the Church, so that that Name, like the oil on Aaron's beard, which ran down to the skirts of his clothing, descends to the humblest and feeblest member of His society. But, alas! now-a-days, heretics tear the robe in pieces, the covetous steal it, the ambitious trample on it, the hypocrites defame it, and the evil lives of Christians pollute it. S. Cyprian says, We may truly say that CHRIST'S robe, without seam and woven throughout, is the Catholic Church; which is so united, and knit, and woven with her LORD and Bridegroom, that the great love which exists between them makes them one.

S. Bede observes, The Scripture does not say that CHRIST'S coat was sewn up and stitched together, but that it was one entire piece of weaving. So let us understand thereby that the SON of GOD embraces and unites to Himself all His elect, insomuch that they become precious threads of His coat, each in its place, each necessary for the completion of the web, each adding to the strength and unity of the texture. And S. Jerome, commenting on Amos, writes: For Holy Scripture to say that the coat was without seam, is to let us know that the bond of love between CHRIST and every fibre of His Church is so close and inviolable, that none can part it or dissolve it. "Who shall separate us from the love of CHRIST? Shall tribulation, or distress, or persecution, or famine, or nakedness, or peril, or sword? ... I am persuaded that neither death, nor life, nor Angels, nor Principalities, nor Powers, nor things present, nor things to come, nor height, nor depth, nor any other creature, shall be able to separate us from the love of GOD, which is in CHRIST JESUS our LORD" (Rom. viii. 35, 38, 39).

S. Ambrose says, It is to be observed that the seamless robe fell not to a Jew, but to a Gentile, and to him by lot, to let us understand that all the merit of the Blood of CHRIST would fall by lot to the Church, and that it was lost to the Synagogue. It is also to be observed that the coat became the property of one soldier by lot; not by any claim of this individual, but by chance. Now that which human wisdom calls chance, Holy Scripture calls Providence or Grace, which determines according to GOD'S foreknowledge and election, not according to man's merit. And so it was through no deserving of us Gentiles that the Grace of GOD and the blessings of His Church fell by lot to us, but rather through the fall of the Jews has salvation come to the Gentiles. "Behold therefore the goodness and severity of GOD: on them which fell, severity; but toward thee, goodness, if thou continue in His goodness: otherwise thou also shalt be cut off" (Rom. xi. 22).

We may well say, that what the world calls chance is really the determinate Counsel of GOD. To the world it may seem chance that we have received the inheritance, but S. Paul says that GOD "hath chosen us in CHRIST before the foundation of the world, having predestinated us unto the adoption of children." That is to say, we are brought into the Church and become Catholics; but let no man think it attributable to his own wisdom, diligence, and deserving; but it is owing solely to GOD'S Grace, which gives, as it were, by lot unto whom He will, and when He pleases, and how He lists. And to the same purpose the Apostle, writing to the Colossians, bids them give thanks to GOD the FATHER for having given them a hope laid up in Heaven, to which they had been admitted, not of their merits, but by the Loving-kindness of GOD.

There is no man to whom there does not fall either good or evil in life, either happiness or sorrow, all which we call our lot, but which is no chance, has been deliberately appointed to us by GOD, and not by accident, but of purpose.

We have already spoken of Joseph's coat of many colours, how that the brothers took it from Joseph and steeped it in the blood of a goat, and then tore it and exhibited it to their father as a token that his son had been devoured by wild beasts. It may be observed, in touching on the history of Joseph, how one sin leads on to another. "One deep calleth another," says David: as one wave rolling on seems to summon the next billow to follow, so does one sin draw on a succession of sins. The brothers envied Joseph, from envying they grew angry, in anger they laid hands on him, then they sold him as a slave, and lastly they lied to their aged father.

In the same way did one sin lead to another when our first parents fell. S. Augustine notes the succession thus: First they sinned in beholding the tree, then from beholding grew desire, from desire came speech, from speech consent, from consent the taking of the fruit, from the taking the eating, from the eating shame and death.

Oh, with what great reason, says S. Cyril, may we ask the Eternal FATHER whether this be the Church without seam which CHRIST left us, when it is so different in appearance from what it was, now the false brethren have torn it, infidels have divided it, heretics have befouled it, and, we may say, this can not be the seamless robe that CHRIST left us. The coat which was shown to Jacob was, however, the very coat that Joseph wore, but after it had been taken from Joseph, it had been rent and steeped in the blood of a goat; and when the unity of the Church, as bequeathed by CHRIST to us, is shown before the FATHER, will not it too appear rent, and tattered, and stained?

S. Jerome says, Heretics destroy CHRIST'S coat without seam by their opinions, princes tear it with their irreverence, Christians divide it with their quarrels, and the clergy cast lots on it with their ambition.

"These things therefore the soldiers did," says S. John. And S. Bede interprets these words thus: For Scripture to tell us that the garments of CHRIST fell to the possession of soldiers, is to let us understand that the reward of His death, and the spoils of His Passion do not fall to those at ease and in pleasure, but to soldiers who war against vices. For, as Job tells us, man's life is a warfare here on earth. "Fight the good fight of faith," is the exhortation of the Apostle; for we Christians are soldiers fighting for a crown against deadly foes.

S. Isidore, in his book, "De Summo Bono," says, Seeing that every day, every hour, and every moment—ay, and in every place, the Devil fights with us with his slights and subtleties, the World with its delights, the Flesh with its pleasures; tell me, is not he who strives against them a true soldier?

There is no earthly war which may not end in peace, or be suspended by a truce; but the war we have to engage in, ourselves, knows no peace, and admits of no truce, and cannot end whilst life lasts. In this war no blood is shed, but tears flow; the conflict is not without, but within; no visible enemies are slain, but vices are exterminated; no agreements are made with foes, for they must be utterly eradicated. Oh, then, this is a glorious war and a happy battle, which the servant of the LORD wages in his own person; for to him that overcometh is given the crown of life and a white and seamless robe!

Remigius says, It wants not a mystery, that the coat without seam was not divided, but fell whole unto him who obtained it by lot; for thereby we may learn that glory and everlasting felicity admits of no division, but that he who obtains it has it whole and entire, and he who loses it loses it altogether. What does he gain who gains this, but to live for ever in Heaven and enjoy the fruition of the Divine essence? And what does he lose who loses this, but to abide for ever in darkness and sorrow? Let our conclusion be, that as he who is not engaged in battle deserves not the spoil, nor the crown of victory; so he who does not fight the good fight against the World, the Flesh, and the Devil, deserves not the garment of CHRIST. In works of virtue, if we can not do all we ought, yet we must do what we can, "and having done all—stand."

CHAPTER XXII.

The Passers-by.

"AND they that passed by railed on Him, wagging their heads, and saying, Ah! Thou that destroyest the temple, and buildest it in three days, save Thyself, and come down from the Cross. Likewise also the chief priests mocking said among themselves with the scribes, He saved others; Himself He cannot save" (S. Mark xv. 29—31).

All conspired together to scoff at CHRIST—the ordinary passers by, the soldiers who watched Him, the thieves who suffered with Him, the lawyers who were present, the priests who had clamoured for His death—so that the whole of Jerusalem was inculpated. Every man stepped out, as it had been in a drama, with some words of blasphemy; every man thinking himself happy if he could cast something in the SAVIOUR's teeth. Some said that He could not save Himself, others bade Him descend from the Cross and they would believe, others derided Him with His claim to be the SON of GOD.

S. Hilary says, That when the Maker of the World was crucified, some blasphemed Him from their hearts, others insulted Him so grievously, that they omitted no injury they could do Him, no torment they could give Him, no false witness they could bring up against Him. S. Augustine likens them to Samson's foxes, wily and subtle, and ready for mischief, fastened together by their tails, bearing destruction among the standing corn, the wheat of the firstfruits.

Tell me, I pray you, what did those children of the Synagogue omit which they could do to humiliate and torture the SON of

God? His life the executioner bereft Him of by the nails, His fame the priests obscured with their tongues, His doctrine heretics defame with their heresies. Of all CHRIST'S possessions here He was robbed, for He had nothing which thieves did not steal.

"As for Me, I am a Worm, and no man : a very Scorn of men, and the Outcast of the people," says the Prophet in the Person of CHRIST (Ps. xxii. 6). That is, I am so disfigured on this Cross, and My body is so bruised and wrenched asunder, that I am like a poor worm that has been trampled on, the lowest and basest of GOD'S creatures, and not like man, the head of creation. I am made an object for jests and blasphemies, I am a very scorn of men, and here on Calvary, without the gate, am I an outcast of the people.

S. Jerome, writing on the Prophet Jonah, makes the striking parallel between Jonah's gourd and the great overgrowth of the old Mosaic law with its vast traditional additions and its cumbrous ceremonial fruit ; and he says, That as in one night that gourd was smitten and died, so now, in the darkness that prevailed from the sixth to the ninth hour, He who was "a Worm and no man," smote that vast plant and wrought its destruction.

"All they that see Me laugh Me to scorn : they shoot out their lips, and shake their heads," continues the Psalmist. That is to say, All those who looked on Me as I hung on the Cross, mocked Me, blaspheming Me with their words and with their gestures, desiring to let all understand by their contemptuous acts and speeches, that they regarded My life as one of folly, and My death as fruitless.

The Prophet David and the Evangelist John meet in this prophecy, for what David foretold, S. John saw with his eyes.

It is natural for one man to have compassion on another, even though that other be his enemy. Thus David mourned for Saul, and Cæsar wept over Pompey ; indeed, the heathen philosopher Seneca says, That it is the part of a reasonable man to pardon him who is humbled before him, and to have compassion for him in his death.

The SON of GOD, however, is the One over whom none felt compassion, and no sympathy was excited, saving only by His

Mother, S. John, and the women who stood afar off. It is usual at an execution for some words of pity to escape the lips of the beholders, some words of encouragement to be offered, some token of humanity to be exhibited, if only some exclamation such as, The GOD of Abraham comfort thee, the GOD of Isaac direct thee, the GOD of Jacob forgive thee! But in this case none spake thus: all the words spoken were bitter words, "yea, they were very swords."

O children of furies, and ministers of hell! such infamous slanders, such malicious speeches, such injurious words, such insulting gestures as ye indulge in, if they are not proper to be used to the living, how much less to the dying?

"He giveth His cheek to him that smiteth Him: He is filled full with reproach" (Lam. iii. 30). He is despised, rejected, scorned; ignominy is heaped upon Him in every form, till He is filled as a vessel to the brim.

Make haste, O ye Jews (says Remigius), make haste with your reproofs and rebukes, for the more you insult Him, the more our reproach diminishes. The Devil would have persuaded CHRIST to cast Himself from the pinnacle of the temple; and Satan's children now would have Him come down from the Cross, that they might see and believe! O deceitful Israelites! exclaims S. Augustine, why do you lie so openly in saying that you will believe when you see Him descend from His Cross? You will not believe though One—even He—rise from the dead, how would you believe this lesser miracle for which ye clamour? O ye Jews, the salvation of the world doth not consist in forsaking the Cross, but in clasping it; not in beginning to suffer, but in enduring to the end; not in sipping the cup, but in drinking it even to the dregs.

Crucified JESUS, we love Thee! Crucified, we adore Thee! Crucified, we believe in Thee! Crucified, we glory in Thee! O Love of our souls, with Thy Cross Thou didst scale Heaven, vanquish the world, triumph over the Devil, make an end of sin, plant Thy Church, and bury the Synagogue. I do not bid Thee then come down from Thy Cross, but cling to it, till all is finished.

S. Anselm exclaims, O excommunicated Jerusalem, O unfortunate people of Jewry! tell me, I pray you, why do you mock at Him and deride Him Who redeems you? JESUS weeps over thy walls, it pitied Him to see Jerusalem in the dust; and dost thou scoff at His precious flesh and holy words? He wept over thy future destruction, dost thou laugh over His? And instead of asking Him to take thee up on the Cross to Him, dost thou bid Him descend to thee?

CHAPTER XXIII.

The Darkness.

"NOW from the sixth hour there was darkness over all the land unto the ninth hour" (S. Matt. xxvii. 45), for the sun hid his face, the moon withdrew her beams, and the stars veiled their burning eyes. Children weep at the death of a parent, servants put on mourning at the decease of their master. Thus these speechless creatures of GOD testify by mourning their sorrow for the death of their Creator.

Angels weep for their Sustainer, the disciples for their Master, men for their Redeemer, creation for its Maker. CHRIST died that He might remit the sin which had brought creation into the bondage of corruption; and therefore creation is agitated with horror, and quakes with amazement, and trembles with hope, knowing that with that death will begin its release and restoration to the glorious liberty of the children of GOD.

S. Chrysostom says, If, as our LORD gave licence to the heavens to darken, and the earth to quake, He had likewise given them liberty to chastise those who slew Him, the heavens would have rained fire and brimstone, and the earth would have opened her mouth and swallowed up those murderers. But though it was His pleasure that His life should end, He would not that His mercy should end: therefore He suffered the elements to be troubled in order to alarm the guilty, but He did not allow them to punish them.

"I call heaven and earth to witness against you this day, that ye shall soon utterly perish from off the land whereunto ye go over Jordan to possess it; ye shall not prolong your days upon it, but shall utterly be destroyed. And the LORD shall scatter you among the nations, and ye shall be left few in number among the heathen, whither the LORD shall lead you!" cried Moses (Deut. iv. 26, 27); and again, "Give ear, O ye heavens, and I will speak; and hear, O earth, the words of my mouth. . . . Do ye thus requite the LORD, O foolish people and unwise?" (Deut. xxxii. 1, 6.)

Moses, before leaving the people whom he had led up out of Egypt, bids them remember that he has set before them life and death, blessing and cursing: that he has warned them, if they rebel against the LORD, they will be overtaken by the curse and death; but if they are obedient, they shall receive the blessing and life. And then he calls on heaven and earth to witness what he has said, and to bear their testimony both to the threat and to the promise.

One thousand, six hundred, and eighty-four years had elapsed since Moses summoned those witnesses, and now they remember the summons; and they lift up their testimony, the heavens by becoming dark, and the earth by quaking. As there were no other witnesses likely to exist till the fulfilment of the prophecy, Moses was constrained to call upon these. Two false witnesses had the Jews suborned against CHRIST, and now two true witnesses testify against them, that, having life and death before them, a blessing and a curse, they have deliberately chosen death and the curse; and therefore, as Moses had threatened, they should be scattered among the nations, and left few in number among the heathen.

S. Jerome says, That the darkening of the sun, the quaking of the earth, the rending of the rocks, the rising of the dead, signified the innocency of CHRIST and the exceeding malice of the people who put Him to death, the injustice and malignity of which act made all creation to stand aghast.

S. Cyprian observes, The earth quaked, the heavens were afraid, hearing the voice of the SON of GOD at the separation of the soul from the body; meaning thereby to let us understand that they could not tacitly endure the death of that their GOD.

Where art thou, O my soul? Dost thou sleep or wake, O my

heart? And dost thou make no reckoning that He is slain and put to death for Thee? The heavens veil themselves in sackcloth, though they were not redeemed; and dost thou regard this awful tragedy with indifference, O my soul, which is being enacted for thy restoration?

Remigius says, That we should make small account of the scoffing of Gentiles at our belief, or the slanders of Jews against our law, for we have two enduring witnesses, Heaven and Earth, that are most true, testifying that the Jew has cast himself away, that the law of Moses is fulfilled, and that the SON of GOD has died to redeem us with His precious Blood. Would they not, think you, bear witness more readily to what the Redeemer did on the Cross, than to what Moses spake on the plains of Moab?

"Sun, stand thou still upon Gibeon; and thou, Moon, in the valley of Ajalon!" (Josh. x. 12) was the adjuration of Joshua. It was as though he said, I require thee, O Sun, in the Name of the GOD of Israel, that thou stand still, and stir not from thy place until I have ended the battle with my enemies, and obtained victory over them. For if the day ends and the night shows herself, they will escape my pursuit.

The prayer of the great captain was of much efficacy. It was more than fulfilled. "The sun stood still, and the moon stayed, until the people had avenged themselves upon their enemies." It is to be noticed that the LORD regards the intent of the heart rather than the words uttered. Joshua prayed, not in the temple, but in the field; not meditating, but fighting; not on his knees, but in his stirrups; not entreating, but conjuring; not asking for ordinary matters, but for miraculous intervention.

Why did our LORD GOD make the day longer when Joshua fought, and shorter when CHRIST died? Joshua shed the blood of the Canaanites on Gibeon, and the Jews shed that of CHRIST on Calvary. Why at Joshua's petition did GOD turn night into day, and at the death of His SON turn the day into night? The secret of this mystery is, that Joshua fought in the service of GOD, whilst the Jews fought against GOD. Joshua fought for the holy Law, the Jews used violence against the Lawgiver. Therefore our LORD, being the Eternal Goodness, gave them no more light to help them in their wickedness. It is to be observed that the darkness cast over the Jews lasted three hours, and the light given to Joshua continued a whole day; wherein we are given to understand how short and mild GOD is in punishing, and how bountiful and liberal He is in rewarding.

There was darkness in Egypt before the death of the firstborn, and the escape of Israel from bondage. So now that the Only-begotten SON of GOD is to die, the preternatural darkness sets in. In order to give token that the bondage is broken, and that the release of the elect is about to take place, that which had happened of old in Egypt recurs again on Calvary.

When Israel had been oppressed in Egypt, GOD brought darkness over the land, and after that released Israel, and destroyed Pharaoh and his host.

When CHRIST had been rejected and crucified by the Jews, GOD again brought darkness over the land, a token that the true Israel after the spirit, and not after the flesh, should be freed from their bondage, and that Jerusalem which had persecuted CHRIST should be overwhelmed in destruction.

When the Church has gone through the last awful trial, when the Antichristian world comes to believe in CHRIST, then again " shall the sun be darkened, and the moon shall not give her light;" a sign for the elect to rejoice and lift up their heads, for their redemption draweth nigh, as also that the Holy One will destroy Antichrist and his host with the breath of His mouth.

Rupert of Deutz says, If we compare the sin of the Egyptians with that of the Jews, we shall find that the latter were the most grievous offenders; and yet in Egypt the darkness lasted three days, whilst on Calvary it continued but three hours. By this JESUS shows how much greater pity He has for men than they have for Him. The Jews cruelly entreated Him, and He gave them three hours of deprivation from light; whilst the Egyptians, ill-treating His chosen people, were punished more severely. He showed Himself rigorous to the Egyptians, that we might understand how much more ready He is to pardon offences committed against Himself than against His Church.

The darkness cast on Egypt was a chastisement, whilst that flung over the Jews was a warning—to these latter it was a foretaste of that outer darkness in which is weeping and gnashing of teeth, into which they would be cast unless they repented. And again, this darkness falling on those who crucified our LORD is a warning to us, that if we crucify to ourselves "the SON of GOD afresh, and put Him to an open shame," the eternal darkness will become our portion.

Because meditation is best conducted in the dark, says S. Hilary, the Divine Providence cast darkness over Jewry, that the faithful who were present on Calvary might ponder on what took place, and the perverse might be enabled to reconsider their purpose, and be brought to repentance.

As the river cannot run, beautifully observes S. Chrysostom, if it is dried at the source, so now the material sun loses his brightness when the Origin of his splendour dies. And S. Anselm points out how the executioners stripped CHRIST of His garments and left Him naked on the Cross; but now the modest sun throws over the unclothed body of the SAVIOUR a veil of thick darkness.

CHAPTER XXIV.

The loud Cry.

"AND JESUS cried with a loud voice, and gave up the Ghost," says S. Mark (xv. 37).

That the SON of GOD with a great cry and many tears did die on the Cross, says Theophylact, is to teach us how to die in the Church, with loud prayer to GOD and tears of contrition for sin.

S. Chrysostom on this place observes, The SON of GOD died on the Cross uttering a loud cry which rang through Heaven, made Hell quake, astonished the Jews, opened the sepulchres, awoke the dead, and converted the centurion.

If all creatures fear Thee, O JESUS, hanging on Thy Cross, who will not fear Thee coming in Judgment? If the Heavens were astonished, and Earth rocked, and Hell quaked at that loud cry, how will they bear to hear that awful word, " Depart, ye cursed"?

The last voice of CHRIST, says Remigius, was a voice full of love, for it proceeded from a loving breast ; it was also a voice full of mystery, for it was the last He uttered.

What death can be likened to that of the SON of GOD, seeing that death came on Him in the embrace of His Cross, with the pardon of His enemies prayed for, with an exclamation on His tongue, a prayer in His mouth, tears on His cheeks, with His Blood exhausted, Redemption accomplished, the Church planted?

The SON of GOD yielded up the Ghost with a strong cry, and this was miraculous, for in the moment of death the voice is weak, as the strength fails. This voice the Holy LORD uttered that all might know that He willingly surrendered His life, and that He feared not death. The SON of GOD yielded up the Ghost when He would, as He would, where He would. By His cry He exhibited His power to lay down His life, and to take it again—and therefore His Godhead; as by His tears He gave evidence of His Manhood. Like a Man He endures the nails, the cross, the spear; like a Man He bears the mocking, the gall, and the vinegar. As GOD, He promises to the thief Paradise, and opens the gates of glory with David's key. That last loud cry summoned the Angels to have compassion on Him, called the elements to cover Him, commanded the sepulchre to receive Him, warned the dead to expect Him; and also it invited the Gentiles who were afar off to draw nigh, being made near by the Blood of His Cross.

S. Chrysostom strikingly observes, He cried with a loud voice as He died. Thenceforth none in His Church can fall away, or none of the heathen can be converted without that call. He that falls away does it wilfully, in spite of the voice. With that loud voice CHRIST called the living and summoned the dead, bidding all be present and testify that He, the GOD of the living and the dead, died both for the quick and dead. Woe be it unto thee, O my heart! woe be it unto thee, O my soul! if thou hear not that call; if that voice speak and thou dost not answer; if it plead and thou turnest a deaf ear; if it cry out and thou dost not awake from the lethargy of indifference in which thou liest!

He cried with a loud voice, because He so rejoiced to see His FATHER satisfied, the world ransomed, the Devil vanquished, Hell spoiled. That loud voice published His joy, for it was the shout of victory.

For whom, asks S. Bernard, did He cry with a loud voice, but for His elect? He could not embrace them, for His hands were nailed; He could not seek them, for His feet were fast; He could not visit them, for He was crucified: but with a loud cry He bid them come, for all things were now ready; Redemption now was theirs.

Oh, infinite Charity! what couldst Thou do more, or what didst Thou leave undone that might profit me? Now with the triumph shout Thou dost crush the Serpent's head, Thou dost open

Heaven, Thou dost seal the testament. Weeping and crying He entered this world in the stable of Bethlehem; and now with tears and "strong crying unto Him that is able to save Him," He departs, His work accomplished, the battle over, the victory won, the world ransomed, pardon secured, Hell closed, sin atoned for, justice satisfied. O Sweet JESUS, great is Thine accomplished work. By the death Thou didst die for me, by the bitter trance Thou passedst through, by Thy loud and bitter cry, I beseech Thee stand by me and sustain me in that hour of dread when Thou shalt call me.

CHAPTER XXV.

The bowed Head.

"HE bowed His head, and gave up the Ghost," says S. John (xix. 30). At the hour that His holy Soul departed out of His body, He bent His head. This incident is full of mystery.

S. Cyril says, That until the SON of GOD ascended the Cross, no command of His FATHER was imposed upon Him, except only that He should be Incarnate; but that after this He was commanded to die, and therefore the Blessed JESUS, not being able to answer with His lips, signed His readiness to obey by an inclination of the head. "He became obedient unto death, even the death of the Cross" (Phil. ii. 8). In obedience He took on Him flesh, in obedience He was born, and in obedience now He dies.

The words of the Apostle indicate the constant obedience of the SON of GOD, which lasted through life to death.

S. Cyprian says, That when the FATHER bade the SON yield up His life, He bowed His head in token of obedience, and at once expired. Happy is the soul which through life, and at the last hour, bows ready to obey the will of the Heavenly FATHER!

It is also to be observed that above CHRIST'S head was the title which Pilate had put upon the Cross, and that in bowing His head our LORD removed it from the title. What harm was there in this title, that CHRIST withdrew His head from it when He was dying? What is more coveted in this world than this title which our LORD resigns? On it was written His kingly Name; and are not royalty, name, position, rank, the things that men seek above all?

What means then this, that CHRIST is lifted up as King, crowned as King, robed as King, saluted as King, and yet puts the title of King from above His head? S. Bernard answers, The SON of GOD would not have this title of honour when He yielded up His Spirit, to give us to understand that His Kingdom was not of this world, and that such kingdom as was offered Him of the tyrant Pilate He put away from Him. Pilate gave CHRIST the title, but CHRIST would not accept the honour at his hands; for though the title was good and just, yet the intention wherewith it was offered was evil and false.

S. Cyprian says, For the SON of GOD to consent that they should put the title of King above His head, and yet withdraw His head from it when He was dying, was to teach us that if it is lawful to retain human and worldly dignities in life, it is advisable to lay them aside voluntarily before death. It is not well to die encumbered with them, lest we seem to relinquish them only on compulsion; but willingly to lay them aside before death, in order to be able with leisure to prepare for it.

CHRIST would not die, says Remigius, with the honour that Pilate gave Him in jest; and darest thou to die in the offices of honour which thou labourest in earnest to procure? S. John Damascene notes, When the Redeemer of the World was about to give up the Ghost, He did not withdraw His shoulder from the cross, nor His hands from the nails, nor His feet from the cords, nor His throat from the halter, nor His heart from the spear, but only His head from the title of King, thereby to teach us that the true servants of the LORD should esteem the injuries and sufferings inflicted on them by the world as honours, but that the honours offered them by the world they should despise. And S. Anselm warns all servants of the Cross to take notice of this action of our Blessed LORD, as it instructs them that their lot is not to be one of honour here, but of shame; not one of pride, but of humility; not one of lordship, but of servitude; not one of mastery, but of obedience.

S. Cyril observes, The nearer the Redeemer drew to His

death, the more and greater were the miracles He wrought. In suffering His side to be pierced, He exhibited His charity; in tasting the vinegar and gall, He evinced His abstinence; in not descending from the Cross when bidden, He showed His constancy; in not answering the railings of His enemies, He gave token of His patience; and the bowing of His head witnessed to His obedience. He stops not His ears against blasphemies they speak; He shuts not His mouth at the vinegar and gall they offer; He withdraws not His side from the thrust of the spear; He resists not the thorns they twine about His brow; He withholds not His hands and feet from the nails with which they pierce them; He keeps not from their scourges His back which they would lacerate: the only thing He refuses is the title of honour which they exhibit above His head.

KING of Kings and LORD of Lords is He called in Holy Scripture; yet He now refuses the name of King, and the LORD is made to die the death of a slave. But He will not take the title and lordship offered Him by Pilate; for His rank and office come to Him, not by man or through man, but are His own by right of His Divinity.

Observe the fickleness of the World. Pilate gives CHRIST the title of King, and crucifies Him as a thief. Observe also the emptiness of the World's honour. Pilate gives the title of King to CHRIST, but keeps the power in his own hands. So does the World bestow on such as follow it the care and the charge of honour, whilst it reserves the gain to itself.

Take heed, O thou ambitious man, how thou receivest honour at Pilate's hands, for that which he gives thee is not fame, but infamy; not honour, but dishonour; not fruit, but leaves; not flour, but bran; not gold, but dross; not reality, but a dream; not a kingdom, but an empty title. And at one time he gives it thee, at another he crucifies thee; or rather, offering thee honours, with them he makes thee accept a cross.

S. Ambrose is of opinion, That CHRIST got more honour by refusing the title than by accepting it; for, he says, he who deserves honour, and has heart and mind sufficiently noble to despise it, is far more to be reverenced than he who obtains it.

In conclusion, the title was given to JESUS, and by JESUS for a while borne with, but was rejected at last. Let His servant so live that in all men's judgment he may deserve respect, and yet deserving it, let him hold it cheap; deserving it by goodness, rejecting it through humility.

CHAPTER XXVI.

The rent Veil.

"AND the veil of the Temple was rent in twain from the top to the bottom" (S. Mark xv. 38). At the very instant that the Soul of CHRIST left His body, the great veil which hung before the Holy of Holies, dividing it off from the Temple, was riven from the top to the bottom without human instrumentality. In the Temple there were two veils; one at the entry, the other concealing that portion which in a church would be called the chancel, but which was called the Holy of Holies. Into this portion those in the body of the Temple could not see, on account of the great veil. It was this veil which was rent.

The first miracle the SON of GOD wrought in His life, was the turning the water into wine at Cana. The first He performed after His death was the tearing of the sanctuary veil. And this He did with greater solemnity than the first, because He did this in His absence, whilst the other He performed in presence; this in the Temple, that in the house; this when dead, the other when living.

From the time that CHRIST was born, to the time that He wrought the miracle at Cana, was thirty years; between that time and this, three years had elapsed; and from the time that He died till the veil was rent, there passed not a minute. In this miracle He showed His power in rending the curtain, His wisdom in doing it at such a time, His immortality in doing it after His death.

Do not think, O Jew! exclaims S. Augustine, that in the SON

of GOD the Divinity died with the Humanity; for though His life had reached its term, His power was unlimited. If thou thinkest that as a Man He hangs on the Cross, learn from the rending of the veil that He is GOD All-powerful still.

S. Jerome explains the rending of the veil thus: That veil prevented entry into the Holy of Holies. By tearing it, GOD let us understand that the sin of our first parents, which kept Heaven shut, was divided betwixt CHRIST and us; and the manner of the division was thus—the fault was ours, the penalty was His. But Agmon has a different and very ingenious interpretation. As it was of necessity (he says) that the veil should be rent or taken away before the Jew could enter into the Most Holy Place, even so, in order that we may enter Heaven, it behoved CHRIST to be divided; that is to say, that the veil, which is His flesh, should be parted; and that He should leave one portion, the body, in the grave, and that the other, the Soul, should rest in Paradise.

S. Ambrose observes; When the Prophet Ezekiel saw one wheel within another wheel, it signified that the Church was involved in the Synagogue. The dividing of the veil was the separation of the Church from the Synagogue, and of the Synagogue from the Church.

When Moses came down from the Mount, he put a veil over his face. When the Israelites received the Law, he spake through the covering without their seeing his face. This veil over the glorious face of Moses signifies that the mysteries of Holy Scripture were hidden and concealed from those living under the Old Dispensation; and to the Jews remaining still in unbelief that veil remains, as S. Paul tells us, untaken away. Isaac's eyes were dark, the eyes of Jacob became dim, Moses wore the veil, Tobit had a whiteness in his eyes, and the children of Israel throughout their history had ever the veil of ignorance and the darkness of unbelief before their faces, and obscuring their vision.

But now CHRIST rends the veil from the top to the bottom. The mysteries of the Old Testament are laid open to us. The Evangelist does not without cause tell us, that all the veil was torn from the highest to the lowest portion; for no secret of the

Old Testament, however high, however low, is not made clear to us, nor is any mystery unfulfilled.

As the veil was slit, one portion fell on one side, the other portion fell back to the other, leaving the centre open. He to whom one portion of the dark veil fell was the Jew; he to whom appertained the other portion was the Heathen; but the Christian, standing on the threshold of the Holy of Holies, sees clearly into the mysteries of Revelation. Let the Jew blindfold his eyes with one tattered fragment, let the other hang over the bewildered Gentile, for we Christians will have no part of it, but only the opening made between the pieces, through which we will contemplate the wondrous things of GOD'S Law. The rending of the veil began from the top, to let us understand that the holy mystery of our Redemption began in the Godhead and ended in the Manhood of CHRIST.

"Verily Thou art a GOD that hidest Thyself," said Isaiah (xlv. 15). He appeared to Moses in a cloud and thick darkness on Sinai, He spake to the Israelites out of the cloudy pillar, He passed in a still small voice before Elijah. To Daniel He appeared in a flame, and the place of the Shekinah was hidden by a veil. But if the Synagogue complain, "Thou art a GOD that hidest Thyself," the Church says with S. John the Divine, "That which was from the beginning, we have seen with our eyes, we have looked upon, and our hands have handled. For the Life was manifested, and we have seen it." We have seen Him without fire, and cloud, and thunderings, but in His flesh; and we have seen His glory. What is there in GOD that He has not revealed unto us? Would we behold His power?—we look upon the world He made. Would we know His doctrine?—we read the Gospel. Would we see His form?—we look upon the body that hangs upon the Tree. Would we learn His secrets? —the veil is rent and all made plain. That which was hid from the wise and prudent is now revealed unto babes.

Would we see CHRIST face to face, says S. Bede, it is necessary for us to take away the veil which is on our hearts and minds; and that veil is sin, which prevents us from seeing CHRIST, and Him from beholding us. "When it shall turn to the LORD, the veil shall be taken away," says the Apostle (2 Cor. iii. 16).

The rent Veil.

First the heart must turn to GOD, and then GOD will tenderly lift and remove the veil that darkens it. The taking away lies in GOD's hands, but it is in man's own power to turn to the LORD.

Wondrous mystery is it, that the net cast into the sea did not break, though filled with a great multitude of fishes; whereas this veil was riven, without a hand laid on it.

The threads composing the veil were the Judaic sacrifices; the cords of S. Peter's net were the Sacraments of the Gospel. The net cast into the sea, dripping with water, enclosing fishes, remained firm, no mesh untied, no cord snapped, no knot unloosed; and so, however much persecution may try, and heresies may strain the texture of the Catholic Church, she will remain whole and entire. Oh, happy the soul that enters that net, and wraps itself in the Sacramental cords! The death of CHRIST, which dissolved the Judaic veil, has braced these bands and secured them for ever.

O Good JESUS, with all humility I pray Thee, that Thou wilt take from off my heart the veil of shame, to the end that I may confess my sins; the veil of malice, that I hurt no more my neighbours; the veil of ignorance, that I may attain Thy secrets; for if Thou wilt not take the veil away, my eyes will close for ever in darkness. I am Isaac, too blind to see the true Jacob; I am Jacob, with eyes too dim to discern Benjamin; I am Tobias, darkened that I cannot see the light of heaven; I am Eli, who cannot see the light in the Temple: and this blindness is fallen on me because I have fallen from Thy Grace. Rend, then, O Good JESUS, the veil of my fault; rend the veil of my malice, the veil of my ignorance; for under all these heavy and thick veils I am shut out from the light of Thy presence, and the prospect of future glory.

CHAPTER XXVII.

The rent Rocks.

"THE earth did quake, and the rocks rent," says S. Matthew (xxvii. 51). The dying voice of the SON of GOD was so terrible, as He surrendered His Soul into the hands of His FATHER, that the earth trembled, and the rocks clave asunder, the sepulchres opened, and many holy men, after the Resurrection, arose from the dead.

There appeared signs and tokens of many kinds, and of divers nature at the death of CHRIST. The heavens became dark, the veil of the Temple was torn, the earth quaked, the mountains shook, and the rocks were rent; these were all testimonies to the power of Him Who died, and to the extent to which His Blood would stream—to the Angels to refresh, to the Jews to redeem, to the Gentiles to convert, to the dead to ransom.

Thirty-and-three years did the SON of GOD live among men on earth, teaching in the Temple, praying upon the rocky mountains, walking the earth, seeking the lost sheep; and now the earth He trod trembles with emotion at His death, the rocky mountains cleave with sorrow, and the Temple rends its garments in despair, whilst the graves open to receive Him.

S. Augustine says, Who will not fear the Cross, and wonder to see CHRIST crucified? for the rocks are riven with fear, the graves gape in dismay! The elements conceived fear, O Good JESUS, which they exhibited by becoming troubled; the stones showed their fear in breaking; the earth gave token of its fear in quaking; the graves evinced their fear by opening. Fear fell on the Jews at these portents; fear possessed the Devil at these

The rent Rocks.

tokens, for now they beheld a dry tree triumph over death, and a dead Man conquer the grave.

Had not the elements reason to be astonied and moved, seeing him killed who was wont to kill, and him triumphed over who was wont to triumph, and him buried who was wont to bury—to see that Death, which was the end of all, itself made an end of?

S. Jerome says, in one of his Homilies, Since the beginning of the world Death was never put to death till now that CHRIST vanquished him and brought into subjection all his power and might; for the triumph CHRIST won over him on the Altar of the Cross was so great, that at the very moment that CHRIST'S Soul left Him, Death lost his reign.

O Good JESUS, great Redeemer of Israel! What further testimony do we require to the certainty of Thy victory over the grave, than these yawning sepulchres, ready to yield up their dead at Thy command? "How is the gold become dim! how is the most fine gold changed! the stones of the sanctuary are poured out in the top of every street!" is the lament of Jeremiah (Lam. iv. 1). That is to say, What great disaster hath befallen thee, O Jerusalem? For suddenly thy gold has lost its brilliancy, and thy most precious gold, polished and pure, has become tarnished, and the stones of thy Temple are strewed over the earth!

Hugo de S. Victor says, That the gold of the Synagogue became dim when, with her LORD and GOD, she lost her favour; and then was her most fine gold changed, when she became rebellious against GOD; and the stones of her sanctuary were scattered in the streets of the world, when all her children were carried into captivity, and her Temple became a desolation.

And then, as says the gloss of Agmon, in the Church of GOD, the gold becomes dim when the Perfect relax their virtuous actions; and the most fine gold is changed, when the Religious adopt a secular life; and the stones of the sanctuary are poured out, when her members desert the Faith. By stone in Holy Scripture obduracy of heart is often signified. What then is meant by the rending of the rocks at the death of CHRIST, but that the hard Gentile world was to be rent, and was to receive the Gospel? And S. Cyprian has the same idea. He says, That since the Creation no blood that was shed had the efficacy of that which was shed by the SON of Mary on the Cross, for that rent the rocks of Judæa, and clave the hearts of the Gentiles; so that of these, by nature hard and impenitent, GOD raised up children unto Abraham.

Jeremiah did not weep because common metals grew discoloured, but because the most precious gold was tarnished; that is, he bewailed chiefly the darkening of the principal among his nation, the scribes and Pharisees and priests, and this darkening was effected through their impenitence. Had not their faith been dim and their nature changed, the lower order, the stones of the sanctuary, would not have been poured out in the street, and scattered among all nations and in all lands.

Jeremiah did not lament for the fall of the stones from towers and battlements, but for the ruin of those of the sanctuary; for our LORD is much more offended by the sins of Priests and those dedicated to religion, than by those of worldlings. The gold loses its hue, when the Priesthood is obscured by vice; the most fine gold is changed when the Religious are indifferent to their vocation; and the stones are poured out, when ordinary Christians are not built up unto a holy temple on the foundation of the Apostles and Prophets, but are dispersed among the countless schisms which distract Christendom.

Oh, how much more reverence and pity did our LORD find in the hard stones of Calvary, than in the harder hearts of the Jews! Behold these poor rocks! When no man durst confess CHRIST, they open to receive Him. The stubborn Synagogue invites Him to come down from the Cross, but He will not hearken; the dumb stones cry out, fissuring to receive Him, and He will answer their silent petition, and will rest in them till Easter dawn.

Oh, how much greater reason had the SON of GOD to yield to the entreaty of the stones, than to the words of the Jews; for these latter conspired to rob Him of His life, and the poor rocks parted to embrace Him and preserve Him from their fury.

" A new heart will I give you, and a new spirit will I put within you: and I will take away the stony heart out of your flesh, and I will give you an heart of flesh," is GOD's promise by Ezekiel (xxxvi. 26); that is, After many days, which shall be in thy time, O Synagogue, if not in thine, O Church, I will take from My servants their hard and impenitent hearts, and will give them those which are softer and more tender; and I will give them a new spirit, even the Comforter, the SPIRIT of Truth. In these few words our LORD promises many and great favours; and in His death He fulfils His promise, for as the rocks are rent at His passion, so are hearts dissolved, and many that were hard and rebellious are brought to tenderness and obedience. And so will it ever be. The Passion of CHRIST will ever be the great means of rending the stony hearts, and dissolving the hardest and flintiest natures.

GOD and Satan have one office and trade, the making of human hearts. But GOD makes His of flesh, whilst Satan labours to petrify them. Sometimes the stony heart is melted, and, turning to the LORD, becomes flesh; and sometimes also the soft fleshy heart, deserting GOD, is hardened by Satan into stone. Judas in the Apostolic College had once a heart of flesh; but after he had sold CHRIST for silver, it turned to stone. The Apostle Paul had a heart of stone when he went to Damascus to apprehend the Christians; but, on the way, it was converted into a heart of flesh.

What is a heart of flesh, but one that is mild, compassionate, gentle, loving, and charitable? And what is a heart of stone, but one that is cruel, selfish, ambitious, covetous, and dissembling?

Oh, what a great favour GOD grants to man! exclaims S. Basil; when He breaks the hard heart, and makes it soft as wax. For in an obstinate heart He will not dwell, neither will He impart to it His benefits. O Good JESUS, am I not harder than a stone, and more callous than flint? For the strokes of tribulation do not break me, nor the waters of Thy visitations dissolve me. Yet, O LORD, Thy loud and dying voice on Calvary shook earth to its foundation, and shattered the rocks; Thou didst not die for the earth, nor for the rocks, but for me. Therefore, O my SAVIOUR, may that loud and bitter cry shake me, and may it rend the caul of my heart, and break it and melt it, for a broken and a contrite heart, I know, Thou wilt not despise.

If thou, O my heart! hast the nature of flesh, thou wilt feel for the death of thy SAVIOUR, Who feeleth in His Soul for thee; therefore, at His loud cry, awake, tremble, and quaking open to receive thy GOD. The sun waxed dark, the Soul of JESUS fled, the Temple veil was riven, the rocks were rent, the earth quaked, and dost thou, O my soul, remain unmoved?

CHAPTER XXVIII.

The opened Sepulchres.

"YE shall know that I am the LORD, when I have opened your graves, O My people, and brought you up out of your graves, and shall put My Spirit in you, and ye shall live," are the words of GOD, recorded by the Prophet Ezekiel (xxxvii. 13, 14).

This great promise, made so long before, is now fulfilled in the events accompanying the death of CHRIST, and culminating in His resurrection. For now the graves, as was foretold, open, and then those therein will be brought up with the spirit of a new life breathed into them.

We have already said how that after CHRIST died, the first miracle wrought was the rending of the veil of the Temple, the second was the cleaving of the rocks of Calvary, the third was the rising up of the bodies of the Saints.

S. Bernard says, How better can we realize, O Good JESUS, Thy death but by this, that by it the living find pardon, and the dead resurrection? The great conquerors of the world were mighty in taking away life, but they raised none to life. They triumphed by destruction, CHRIST triumphed by restoration.

The glorious Augustine says, What other thing are we given to understand by the opening of the graves wherein are dry bones, but that now those old Scriptures which entombed the dead letter of the Law are opened to all; and life is infused into what was old, and dry, and dusty; and the SPIRIT, breathing upon them, vivifies the sense? As it would be a matter of small profit if the LORD opened the graves and did not send His

SPIRIT to raise up again, the mysteries involved in the letter, so also does it little avail us to turn over the letter of Scripture that He has opened to us, without an infusion of Divine Grace to assist us in understanding what we read.

S. Cyprian exclaims, O Good JESUS, how immediately dost Thou test the power of Thy Blood! for Thou givest Paradise to the thief who hung beside Thee, and unto the dead in the graves around Thee dost Thou communicate life. What is He not able to do, Who gives glory to the living, Who gives life to the dead?

In the prophecy recorded by Ezekiel, it is to be noted that the LORD does not say that any other except Himself shall open the graves, and raise the dead, and give them the SPIRIT; to let us understand that it is He only Who can break the death-like sleep of sin, lift up from an evil habit, pardon and restore, infusing into man that life which is hid with CHRIST in GOD.

It is also to be considered, that our LORD says that He will first open the graves, and then will raise the dead; from which we may gather that the conscience must be first shaken, and the soul opened in confession to exhibit its dead, before the Spirit of Life descends. "Woe unto you, scribes and Pharisees, hypocrites! for ye are like unto whited sepulchres, which indeed appear beautiful outward, but are within full of dead men's bones, and of all uncleanness!" said our Blessed LORD (S. Matt. xxiii. 27). CHRIST despised these painted tombs because of the pollution within. Men are often more eager to know that a friend or kinsman has a decent monument than that his soul should be at rest; they will take greater care to engrave over a corrupting body, at no little expense, the many virtues he possessed in life, than they took in his life to make him acquire these virtues. Little does it matter what or where man's grave may be, if only his soul is well cared for.

Lazarus was cast into the ditch, but his soul was transported by Angels to Abraham's bosom. Dives was buried in a marble tomb, but his soul was borne by Devils to the place of torment.

Pliny, in the Prologue to his Seventh Book, says, Among all creatures created by Nature, man alone weeps, is ambitious, proud, covetous, and, worst of all, makes himself a tomb, and endeavours by fame to prolong his life. Pliny is right. Riches do not elate other creatures, nor do they labour to accumulate treasure; they laugh not when born, nor weep at the approach of death, but labour only to live, not regarding how they may be buried.

S. Gregory says, That a man ought not to calculate how long he may live, but how well he may live; not to have thought concerning the tomb which is to contain his carcass, but whether his soul will enter into rest or not.

S. Jerome, in an Epistle, writes, Do not the labours and cares of the body suffice thee, but must thou take other cares upon thee as well, the care of where thy wearied bones are to lie, and where the worms are to gnaw thy flesh? Better is it to live aright, than to be buried well.

If the Poet do not deceive us, the night that Troy was burnt, when Æneas asked his father Anchises to leave the city lest he should be without a tomb, the old man answered, "Facilis est jactura sepulchri;" that is to say, Among all the calamities and pains of life, the least that man can have is the loss of a handsome tomb. Anchises made a good answer. Men make great disturbance over any trouble that affects them in life; but they are powerless to exhibit emotion at any indignity offered, after death, to their bodies.

If it had been the pleasure of the SON of GOD that we should be careful about our burial, He would have suffered the young man to have buried his father; but, said He, "Let the dead bury their dead." The reverence we show to our fathers is better exhibited in obedience than in pompous funerals.

But to return to our former point.

CHRIST compared the Pharisees to sepulchres, which were without showy and gay, but were within a mass of festering corruption. Thereby He lets us see how He abhors profession which is at variance with practice, and practice opposed to profession.

All the care of the hypocrite is for appearance, but "the LORD trieth the spirits." The hypocrite cares not to deserve, but to appear to deserve; not to be good, but to seem to be good.

The rebuke which the SON of GOD gave to the hypocrites of His day applies to those of our own time also.

What does it avail to deny oneself in trifles of dress and of diet whilst the will remains unsubdued? What does it profit us to use long prayers, if they are only said for a pretence? What does it profit to preach on charity, and to have the heart embittered with envy and hatred? What does it advantage us to advise peace and good-will, if we stir up strife by our unbridled tongues?

S. Gregory, in his Morals of the Book of Job, remarks pithily, That those are whited sepulchres who, to better their own condition, or gain credit among their neighbours, detract from the good of others.

S. Anselm has also a striking remark on the subject. He says: Many a holy body is in a vile grave, and many a wicked body is in a pompous tomb; so, too, there are many in this world whom, by their surroundings, we rashly judge to be worldlings and dissolute; but who, being inwardly known, are holy; and there are many who, by their profession and externals, one would judge to be Saints, yet who, if examined inwardly, would be found to be reprobates.

Open then, O Good JESUS, the sepulchre of my corrupt heart, and draw forth all therein that offends Thee, awake that which slumbers, vivify that which is dead, restore that which languishes, and revive all with the Spirit of life!

Our Blessed LORD calls those who are in guilt dead; but those whom the world regards as dead, He terms sleepers.

Oh, who could be worthy to hear at His blessed mouth the words, "Our friend Lazarus sleepeth;" or, "The maid is not dead, but sleepeth"? for, in the presence of CHRIST'S goodness and charity, he is not dead whom the sepulchre encloses, but only he who is devoid of Divine grace. Better, then, to die in the grace of GOD, and so only to slumber, than to live out of the favour of GOD, and living to be but dead.

O Good JESUS, rend the rocks of my hardness and impenitence, throw down the sepulchre of my hypocrisy, reform the bones of my sins, and sift the ashes of my unruly desires! Raise me up, not from the sleep of death, but from the death of death itself—the death of sin in which I lie a prey to the corruption of my evil nature, and the worm of a perverted conscience.

CHAPTER XXIX.

The Testimony of the Centurion.

"AND when the Centurion, which stood over against Him, saw that He so cried out, and gave up the Ghost, he said, Truly this Man was the SON of GOD" (S. Mark xv. 39). When the Romans had conquered the land of Jewry, the Governor of Jerusalem was given a guard of Roman soldiers, partly for the safe keeping of his person, and partly for the execution of justice. The captain of each hundred men was called a Centurion. One of these Centurions, the captain of those men who had crucified CHRIST, was present to see that the commands of the Governor were executed by the soldiers under him. The Centurion was a Gentile, a servant of the Gentile Emperor, and he himself had the command over a Gentile band of soldiery.

In the name of the Synagogue, the Jews said, "We have no king but Cæsar;" and in the name of the Gentile Church, the Centurion exclaims, "Truly this Man was the SON of GOD." On the same day the Jew rejected CHRIST, and the Gentile received Him. The Synagogue cast Him out, and the Church embraced Him. "The stone shall cry out of the wall, and the beam of the timber shall answer it." The words are those of Habakkuk (ii. 11) the Prophet, speaking of the times of the Messiah, when the city would be established by iniquity, and the town builded with blood, and when the earth would be filled with the knowledge of the glory of the LORD as the waters cover the sea. That is to say, when Jerusalem should shed the Blood of CHRIST, thereby the knowledge of Him would be proclaimed to the ends of the earth.

What is the stone that cries out of the wall, but the Centurion testifying, "Truly this is the SON of GOD!" And what is the beam out of the timber answering that cry, but the title on the Cross, "JESUS of Nazareth, the King of the Jews"?

The great Centurion had the properties of a stone. He was hard with unbelief, heavy with sin, cold with idolatry, and yet, as the rocks rent, he too was shaken, and his hardness dissolved; he saw and believed, and believing he exclaimed, "Truly this was the SON of GOD." He confessed Him to be Man, "This Man." He confessed Him to be GOD, "The SON of GOD." He confessed Him to be just, "Certainly this was a righteous Man." What was there more to be confessed in CHRIST, than this that the Centurion owned?

S. Ambrose says, The confession of the Centurion that the Prophet whom the Jews had put to death was a Man, and GOD, and Just, was perfect: Angels have nothing further to confess, men have nothing more to believe.

S. Leo, in one of his Sermons, remarks, If the Centurion had said, Truly this *is* the SON of GOD! instead of, Truly this *was* the SON of GOD, there would have been nothing further to have been desired in his confession; but, being a novice in the faith, he knew nothing of His coming Resurrection. Therefore he said, He *was*, not He *is*.

This Centurion was no Jew, but a Gentile; no Hebrew, but a Roman; not learned, but simple; and yet, nevertheless, he openly professed CHRIST'S Godhead, and proclaimed His Manhood, and testified to His Righteousness, at a time when the Jews, men of CHRIST'S own nation and kindred, hated His doctrine, defamed His honour, persecuted His followers, crucified His person, and robbed Him of life.

The great accusation brought against CHRIST was, that He made Himself the SON of GOD; and, notwithstanding, the Centurion boldly confesses that "Truly He was the SON of GOD!" that what CHRIST had assumed to be, that He was; that what the Jews had denied Him to be, that was He nevertheless. The Centurion's faith was strong, for he persuaded himself to believe that which he did not see, contrary to what he did see. What he did see, was a Body crucified; what he believed was, that CHRIST was Very GOD.

That which he confessed is highly to be esteemed; but the time at which he spoke makes it the more estimable. For the Centurion spoke out before the Jews who had accused CHRIST, the passers-by who had mocked Him, the thief who had scorned Him, and the soldiers who had crucified Him, restoring to CHRIST His fame, and possibly exposing himself to jeopardy. Had he not been a Roman captain with a hundred men under him, that speech would unquestionably have cost him dear; for by acknowledging the injustice of the sentence pronounced against CHRIST, he ranged all those who had clamoured for it against him, as his enemies, fired with deadly hostility.

Behold! exclaims Remigius, the Blood of CHRIST melts the heart of this Gentile like wax, and petrifies the Synagogue!

When the Redeemer of the World was about to render up His Soul, the last sinner to address Him was the penitent thief; and after His Soul had sped, the first to speak was this Centurion.

The captain of the thieves asked, "LORD, remember me!"

The captain of the soldiers said, "Truly this was the SON of GOD!"

Into Thy hands, O Good JESUS, the thieves commend themselves, with a "Remember me!" And with a "This was the SON of GOD," the soldiers confess Thee.

Surely when we look at Calvary, and see some there believing in CHRIST, yet silent, and this unbeliever suddenly illuminated, and testifying to his faith with a loud voice, we may take the lesson to heart to despair of none, to despise none, for where least expected, and also when least expected, the seed of faith germinates, and the rocky impenitence becomes soft. Among the good wheat springs up the cockle. Yes; but also among the thorns blossom sweet roses.

S. Chrysostom says, The occasion of the Centurion's conversion was the manner in which CHRIST accepted His death. He saw that the LORD took the Cross upon Him without a murmur, did not complain when scourged, nor speak when stripped of His garments; but was meek and gentle as a lamb before his shearers, and crucified, he heard Him praying for His murderers. It was not much preaching, it was not working great works, which so much turned the Roman Centurion, as patient endurance—not active labour, but passive suffering.

S. Gregory says, in his Pastoral, Prelates who rule and govern, and preachers who teach, ought to take example by the conversion of the thief and the confession of the Centurion, both of whom were drawn to CHRIST, not so much by words as by deeds. It is easier to turn men's hearts by example than by much exhortation.

S. Cyril says, The confession of S. Peter was great when he said, " Thou art the CHRIST, the SON of the Living GOD," and that which the Centurion made was great, when he said, " Truly this was the SON of GOD." S. Peter said, Thou art; the soldier, He was; but though the latter was most imperfect in one way, it was more perfect in another; for it was spoken, not like the other, before a select few, but before a vast concourse, not before disciples, but before enemies. This Centurion, the first Gentile who at the Cross confessed JESUS, afterwards was one of the first to receive the crown of martyrdom; thus imitating S. Peter in his confession, and S. Stephen in his death.

CHAPTER XXX.

The smitten Breasts.

"AND all the people," says S. Luke (xxiii. 48), "that came together to that sight, beholding the things which were done, smote their breasts, and returned."

It would have been well for these startled Jews, if the last two words of this verse had been other than they are. It is well that the sight—that spectacle to men and Angels—of the SON of GOD dying for the whole world, should have so astonished them, that they quaked inwardly with the reeling earth, that their hearts should have been rent with the cleaving rocks, that the veil of unbelief obscuring their vision should have been torn and taken away, and that they should be conscious that their hearts were open to yield up the dead imaginings therein, and that they should smite their breasts as they realized that they had crucified the LORD of Glory. All this were well; but it is ill that they should return. On Calvary is the Church; they turn their backs on it to seek the deserted Temple.

It was fear that impelled the Jews to smite their breasts, fear at the sight of the darkness, and the earthquake, and the yawning graves; but it was not repentance. Had they felt compunction, they would have clung to the Cross; but being influenced by a bare fear alone, "they returned."

Robertus, in his Gloss, says, If you would see whether this smiting of the breasts proceeds from compunction or from fear, follow the returning crew, and you will see them enter Pilate's house to ask that the legs of the crucified ones may be broken, and that a watch may be set and the sepulchre secured. "Sir, we remember that that Deceiver said, while He was yet alive, After three days I will rise again. Command therefore that the sepulchre be made sure until the third day" (S. Matt. xxvii. 63). Such wicked words, such shameless requests, are they, think you, such as would proceed from penitent men, or from those hardened in their crime? How could that have been true repentance for the slaying of CHRIST, which sought to restrain Him from rising again? Could there have been contrition in the use of the word "Deceiver"?

It was, says S. Bede, the sight of the awful signs in heaven and earth which produced a panic among them, not dismay at the consciousness of their having acted amiss.

If the Jews would have confessed CHRIST, with the Centurion; or prayed to Him to remember them, with the thief; or gone with Joseph to beg His body; or, with Nicodemus, sought spices wherewith to anoint It—we might have believed that they were penitent, and that the smiting on their breasts was an outward expression of the inward feeling. S. Chrysostom says, If the Evangelist had said they were turned, and not "they returned," we should have believed that the sign of the smitten breasts betokened contrition for their guilty act; but Scripture says "they returned," that is, they turned the same way by which they had come, and a bad way was that. They came in the commission of a sin, they returned with the sin completed; they came seeking the Blood of CHRIST, they returned with that Blood on their heads and on their posterity; they came with hardening hearts, they returned with them permanently hardened.

"The people—who came together to that sight," the sight or spectacle of the struggle between the PRINCE of Light and the Powers of Darkness, now returned: that spectacle which had converted the thief and the Centurion had for ever hardened them.

What spectacle had the Greeks like this at any time? asks S. Chrysostom. What sight like this had the Romans ever in their triumphs? To-day the people crowd to the sight, and what do they see? On the dry wood of the Cross their Synagogue ends, the prophecies are fulfilled, the figures are buried, malice prevails, Innocency is condemned, Spotlessness is executed, the Maker is unmade, and Death is robbed by death of his dominion.

This spectacle is presented to all, and it has two effects, it either softens or it hardens. Every time the Passion of CHRIST is brought before the thought of a Christian, it profits or it harms him. So it is with every sermon that is preached, wherein the Death of the SAVIOUR is presented to the people. Some cry out with the thief to be remembered in His Kingdom; some profess their belief with the Centurion; some are bathed in tears, with pierced soul like Blessed Mary; some derive profit from it like S. John, who by it gained a Mother; and others go away with their hearts deader, colder, more obdurate, than before.

So is it also with the spectacle of the Sacrifice of the Holy Eucharist, wherein CHRIST is evidently set forth crucified among us. Some halt at the outward Element and are offended, others with the eye of faith discern CHRIST and are satisfied.

"They smote upon their breasts." The action was well enough, but there the good stopped. Who could have done greater reverence to CHRIST than Pilate's servants when they bowed the knee before Him, and saluted Him as King? By this thou mayest see, my brother, that true contrition doth not consist in praying with the hat off, in kneeling, in striking the breast, in using right expressions with the lips; but in feeling deep sorrow at heart, and by showing amendment of life. There is nothing wrong or superstitious in striking the breast, in using the sign of the holy Cross, or in kneeling in Church; nay, rather, they are good and excellent customs: but with them we must also amend our lives and repent of our sins, and worship with our spirits, otherwise we shall only obtain credit of men, and receive no reward of GOD. O Good JESUS, Love of my soul! I humbly beseech Thee not to suffer me to be one of these who smite their breasts but do not repent of their sins; but to be one of a broken and contrite heart, such as I know Thou dost not despise!

Do not suffer me, O Good JESUS, to return with the Jews to my house, but make me to persevere on Calvary, and abide with Thy Mother until Thou be laid in Thy grave; for all those that continued with Thee through Thy woes on Good Friday, were comforted by Thee at Thy Resurrection on Easter morning.

Do not suffer me to be one of those who were not converted at the rending of the rocks and the quaking of the earth; but make me one of those who turned to Thee for Thy works and doctrine. Nearest to Thee are drawn those who cleave to Thee through love; more remote are those who turn to Thee through fear.

Who will direct me unto Thy house, who will open me the gate, who will knock for me at the door? unless Thy love guide me, unless Thy love knock for me, unless Thy love open unto me.

Give me, O Good JESUS, give me Thy holy Grace, that I may to Thee open the breast of my desires, and not smite it like the Jews: unless I open, Thou canst not enter; and unless Thou enterest, Thou wilt not take up Thy abode with me; and unless Thou abide with me, I shall go all my days mourning.

CHAPTER XXXI.

The pierced Side.

"ONE of the soldiers with a spear pierced His side, and forthwith came there out blood and water" (S. John xix. 34). According to the desire of the Jews, soldiers were sent to break the legs of those crucified, that they might die before the Sabbath. The soldiers brake the legs of the thieves; but when they came to JESUS they brake not His legs, for He was dead already, thereby unconsciously fulfilling the prophecies. But one of the soldiers, to make sure to the Jews that CHRIST was dead, thrust his lance into His side, and as he drew it forth again, there gushed forth Redeeming Blood and Baptizing Water. Now indeed with the Psalmist we may say, that they vex Him Who has been wounded, and persecute Him Who is smitten; that now indeed has the rebuke of the Eternal FATHER broken His sacred and suffering heart.

Joab "took three darts in his hand, and thrust them through the heart of Absalom" (2 Sam. xviii. 14). Absalom was hanging by his hair in the oak when Joab, the captain of the host, came up; and seeing him thus suspended, he smote him with three spears till he died. The blows of Joab dealt to Absalom wounded the heart of his father David, who, feeling the blow, exclaimed, "O Absalom, my son, my son."

Absalom was the son of a king, and CHRIST was the SON of GOD. Absalom was the fairest of men, and of CHRIST it is said, "Thou art fairer than the children of men; full of grace are Thy lips." Absalom died on an oak; CHRIST was crucified on the Cross. By the death of Absalom the kingdom was pacified, and by the death of CHRIST all the world was redeemed. CHRIST and Absalom were of one lineage and house, and of the same princely tribe. Joab slew Absalom against his father's will, and the SON of GOD was slain by the Jews and His FATHER was grieved thereat. The slaying of Absalom was an act of disobedience, and it was a culminating act of disobedience to slay CHRIST. By the hair of his head Absalom was attached to the oak, and CHRIST was bound to His Cross by the thoughts and purpose of His Divinity; and He was slain by three nails, and pierced with one spear. Absalom died in rebellion against his father, and CHRIST died bearing the rebellion of the people upon His shoulders to satisfy the FATHER, and effect a reconciliation.

Absalom was pierced by three spears, and CHRIST was transfixed with three great woes. The first was the pain He felt in His sacred Body; the second was the anguish of His most holy Soul; and the third was the suffering in His blessed Mind.

The nails, the scourge, the spear, drove home the first great pang. The sight of the weeping Mother and scattered Disciples were the second thrust. The shame of nakedness, the humiliation, the insults, they caused the third and keenest blow. But what drove it to His heart with greatest agony, was the consideration that His death would profit so few; that of the many to whom His Blood would be offered, so few would accept and apply it.

And when the soldier thrust the spear into the side of CHRIST, did he not pierce three hearts at one stroke? The heart of the holy Mother who brought CHRIST into the world, the heart of John the Disciple whom JESUS loved, and the heart of the Magdalen whom He had converted. Joab with three spears smote one heart; this soldier with one spear transfixes three.

Origen remarks on the type we are considering: The hanging of David's well-beloved son on a dry oak was a figure of CHRIST suspended on the rough Cross, on the which He hung rather by the cords of His love, which attached Him to that tree wherewith He would redeem us, than with the nails with which the soldiers made Him fast. From the heart Joab sought the death of Absalom, and from the heart also did the Jews labour to kill CHRIST.

S. Leo exclaims, O Synagogue, how perverse and cruel thou art! The lion that strikes down his prey does not mangle the carcass, but thou dost not spare the body of Him Whose death thou hast wrought. Behold His face so wan and pale, His eyes closed, His bones out of joint, His veins bloodless, His flesh torn, His head bowed; hast thou the cruelty to injure further this Soulless tenement?

O cruel Spear! says S. Anselm, what dost thou seek anew in the sight of my GOD and my CHRIST? If thou seek His Disciples, they have deserted Him; if thou seek His Flesh, it is dead; if thou seek His Blood, it is shed in the streets; if thou seek His garments, they are divided among the soldiers; if thou seek His Soul, it is already gone to His FATHER.

"Make thee an ark of gopher wood . . . a window shalt thou make to the ark, and in a cubit shalt thou finish it above; and the door of the ark shalt thou set in the side thereof" (Gen. vi. 14, 16).

GOD commanded Noah to make the ark of light and buoyant wood, to pitch it within and without with pitch, that no water might enter; and in the side to make a little door, through which alone he might enter or leave the ark.

Although this glorious figure has been often expounded, yet we will seek some further mysteries in it; and if we fail to discover much, it will be through the imperfection of our understanding and the dimness of our eye.

First of all, we say that Noah's ark is our blessed and holy Mother, the Church, out of which is no salvation, as out of the ark was no safety from the flood. The boards of the ark were of light and strong wood, that did neither rot with moisture, nor sink through weight, nor cleave with age, nor yield before the billows. The fabric of the Church is such, that the old gnawing serpent cannot rot its strength away, nor will the waters of tribulation drown it, nor may the winds of prosperity cast it on the rocks.

Now, as in a ship there are many things that properly do not belong to the vessel, so are there in the Church of CHRIST many things and persons which are not of CHRIST. Who is he that is in the ark but is not of the ark, but he who is in the Christian family yet is not a Christian? The wicked Ham was in the ark with Noah, and the traitor Judas was in the Church with CHRIST. In like manner there are many baptized and professing Christians who are not of CHRIST.

As the ark was pitched within and without with pitch, so is the Church made fast by charity, the very bond of peace; within, among those who believe, and without, to those who are not of the Faith; within, to GOD, without, to man.

As in the ark were many small chambers, so in the Church of GOD are there many offices. GOD commanded that the ark should be three hundred cubits long and fifty in height, and thirty in breadth, and that it should be "finished above in a cubit," to let us understand that, however different soever one degree may be from another in the Church of GOD, nevertheless, all are summed up in one, that is, in the belief in One, True, and Only GOD. For all estates and degrees end in one estate and one degree, and all cubits are summed up above in one cubit; for all mount to the One and only Head and King, in "Whom the whole body fitly joined together and compacted by that which every joint supplieth, according to the effectual working in the measure of every part, maketh increase of the body unto the edifying of itself in love" (Eph. iv. 16).

The door at the side of the ark is CHRIST Himself. "I am the Door; by Me if any man enter in, he shall be saved," said our Blessed LORD Himself.

But CHRIST'S natural body is a figure of CHRIST'S Body mystical. His most holy body was framed in the Virgin's womb, tossed on the flood of ungodliness, pitched within and without with perfect charity, illumined from above by the Divine Intelligence, and now is the door made in the side of that ark, whereby all may enter in, and entering may find safety.

S. Augustine says: Do not think that the Evangelist used the word "pierced" by chance, instead of "wounded," for it was rather an opening and unlocking of mysteries by a key, than a wounding with an iron barb.

S. Chrysostom observes: With the waters of the Red Sea the

Egyptians were drowned, and with the blood of the Lamb the Israelites were delivered. So, in like manner, with the Blood of this Holy LAMB was wrought our redemption, and with the Water that flowed from His sacred Side was wrought our purification. The Blood gushed forth to redeem the captive; the Water poured forth to cleanse the defiled.

From the opened side of JESUS flowed two of the blessed Sacraments, Holy Baptism and the most Holy Eucharist. S. Hilary says, That as Eve was formed from the side of Adam in sleep; so from the side of CHRIST slumbering in death was His Bride, the Church, taken.

O sacred Water, flowing from the heart of my LORD and my GOD, cleanse me in thy stream, wash away my offences, purge me of my iniquities!

O sacred Blood, bursting from the heart of my LORD and my GOD, sustain, and strengthen, and restore me!

CHAPTER XXXII.

The Spear.

"AND He spake unto the Man clothed with linen, and said, Go in between the wheels, ... and fill thine hand with coals of fire from between the Cherubim, and scatter them over the city" (Ezek. x. 2). That is, there appeared a vision to the Prophet. He beheld GOD seated upon His throne, and before Him were the Cherubim. And a Man was there in a white linen garment; and to this Man said GOD, Go in between the wheels which are under the Cherubim, and take up a great handful of coals, and cast them over Jerusalem.

Who is signified by the Man in linen raiment, but JESUS CHRIST the SON of GOD, and the SON of Man? He stands between two wheels, that is, His Personality exists in two Natures united in One, the Divine Nature and the Human Nature. Each is represented as a wheel to which is neither beginning or ending, for the Nature of GOD has no beginning, and the nature of Man has no ending. Thus He appears as GOD and Man, GOD of the Substance of the FATHER, begotten before the world; and Man of the substance of His Mother, born in the world, and inseparably and eternally united to it; so that, like Melchizedek, He has neither beginning of days nor end of life, but abideth a Priest for ever; and in this vision His Priesthood is foreshadowed in the linen vesture, in which He went to Calvary to offer His Sacrifice, and in which He still pleads that Sacrifice as Priest in Heaven. "I saw ... in the midst of the seven candlesticks ONE like unto the SON of Man, clothed with a garment down to the foot" (Rev. i. 13).

The SON of GOD was, from the first instant of His conception, between the two wheels. He enjoyed the one, which was His Divine Essence, and tasted of the other, which gave Him the passions and affections of human nature. It does not want in mystery, that the two wheels moved together; whereby we understand that the SON of GOD never did a miracle incompatible with His Human Nature, nor suffer anything to which His Divine Nature did not consent.

"Fill thine hand with coals of fire." What is the signification of this? The burning coals have two natures, they glow with ardour, and they burn the hand that grasps them. The ardour is the love of CHRIST, the suffering that heat produces is the Passion He endured.

It is to be noted, that in Holy Scripture the term "hand" is often applied to the Second Person of the ever Blessed TRINITY. Thus, "Let Thine Hand help me" (Ps. cix. 173). "Send down Thine Hand from above" (Ps. cxliv. 7), which passages refer to salvation through the Incarnation of the SON of GOD. For as the hand proceeds from the arm, and is of one substance and nature with the arm, so did the SON proceed from the FATHER, and is of the same Substance and Nature, though of distinct Personality.

What does it signify, that this One in the linen vesture takes in His hand hot burning coals?—but that He Who is a Priest for ever, in His Priesthood offered Sacrifice; and as the coals burned Himself, so was that Sacrifice a Sacrifice of Himself; and as the manner of the Oblation was that he took hot glowing coals, so did CHRIST through the ardour of His love offer Himself?

What does it signify, that the hand is one and the coals many?—but that the Person of GOD is One, and the coals of torments endured by Him are many; and the pains wherewith He was laden, infinite. Mark how He takes, not a few coals, but a handful; for His love exceeds the love of Angels, and His pain surpasses the pain of Martyrs!

Do you not think that He has His hand full of coals, Who loves thee so well, thou being rebellious; and suffers so acutely for thee, thou being undeserving?

What does it signify, that the coals were of the fire of the

Cherubim which did ever burn?—but that the love which CHRIST bore in His heart was of that glowing fire, which is never extinguished and never wasted.

What does it signify, that the Man in vesture of linen is bidden cast these coals on Jerusalem?—but that the love of CHRIST should be spread abroad throughout His Church.

What does the opening of the hand signify?—but that the heart which contained that glowing love and felt those keen pangs should be opened, and that this opening should be the means of dispersing the burning embers. "I am come to send fire on the earth; and what will I, if it be already kindled?" said our Blessed LORD; and the Baptist foretold that He would baptize with fire; and lo! when the Day of Pentecost was fully come, that storehouse of fire which was opened by the lance on Good Friday scatters its embers in flaming tongues of fire throughout the New Jerusalem of the newly-constituted Church. That fire is love; and its manifestation is suffering. CHRIST'S love for us induced Him to bear His Passion; if we love Him, we shall be called to suffer both with Him and for Him.

Our LORD has many gifts to bestow, and many graces to give; but, as long as life lasts, I will desire of Him only this, the burning coal to consume my vices and to enkindle my love.

O Good JESUS, Love of my soul! seeing Thou dost bid me call, and Thou promisest to answer, Thou dost bid me ask, and assure me that Thou wilt answer, I do not ask of Thee bread, or raiment, or dignity, or pleasure, but only some of Thy coals to burn me; for I know that I shall not obtain Thy graces hereafter, unless Thou first triest with the fire and refinest to perfect.

Open, then, O Good JESUS, open Thy hand, and give me Thy coals, and open Thy heart that I may be enkindled. How can I call myself Thine, unless I be baptized with the Baptism of Fire wherewith Thou art baptized withal? Give me, then, in this life coals to burn me, that in the life to come I may have roses to solace me.

Oh, what a comfort it is, that the Prophet says that our LORD hath not the fire of His love at His feet to spurn it, but in His hand to bestow it.

"The sin of Judah is written with a pen of iron, and with the point of a diamond : it is graven upon the table of their heart, and upon the horns of your altars" (Jer. xvii. 1). S. Jerome, commenting on this passage, supposes that the Prophet is speaking of the sin of idolatry, which could not be blotted out or erased ; but that the more Judæa and Samaria increased, the further they would sink in idolatry, and the more they would forget GOD. But others suppose that Jeremiah looked forward to the last and awful sin of Judah, committed against CHRIST, when, with the iron pen of the spear, they would grave the tablet of CHRIST'S heart, and write on the horns of their altars—on His heart, Love; on theirs, Hate ; on His, Redemption ; on the horns of their altars, Desolation ; and that this writing would be against them to the end of the world.

The sin of Adam was engraven on our hearts ; and although it was redeemed by CHRIST and taken away by Baptism, yet there remains still in us a thousand inclinations to sin, and small strength to resist it. That old sin being deeply graven in our hearts, how should we possibly become virtuous, were it not for the succour of the grace of our LORD ? When Jeremiah speaks of the sin written with a pen of iron, and an adamantine point, so as to be indelible, on our hearts and on our Altars, he refers, in one sense, to the sin of Adam and to the "writing that was against us," the condemnation for sin which was stamped on our actions, our thoughts, our very devotions. But that writing has been effaced. It has been washed away by the Blood of CHRIST, erased by the point of the spear. Jeremiah, and all who lived before the coming of our SAVIOUR, beheld only the handwriting with the iron pen and adamant point, " Lamentations, and mourning, and woe" (Ezek. ii. 10). " GOD hath numbered thy kingdom, and finished it. Thou art weighed in the balances, and art found wanting " (Dan. v. 26, 27); whereas we, who come after, see the sacred Blood of CHRIST blotting it out, and the spear-head erasing it utterly.

If the glorious Apostle Thomas, from being incredulous, became a most faithful Christian, by thrusting his hand into CHRIST'S side, oh, what riches of belief, what store of joy, what abundance of consolation wilt thou not gain if thou wilt enter by contemplation into that sacred heart !

If the great Evangelist, John, by resting on that holy breast obtained greater insight into the Divine mysteries than the other Apostles of the LORD, what wilt thou gain if thou wilt only follow the spear and repose, not on, but in, that opened Breast!

S. Bernard, in his book, "De Planctu Virginis," says: What means this, O JESUS? Is Thy head rent with thorns, Thy hands torn with nails, Thy shoulders opened with the scourge-thongs, and couldest Thou not withhold Thy breast, which alone was entire, but must yield that also to be maimed and wounded, giving Thy consent that the spear should smite and open Thy side and transfix Thy heart?

The thorns, says S. Anselm, met the brain, the thongs reached the bones, the cords scarred the flesh, the nails tore the sinews, but the spear, most happy, met and penetrated the heart itself, the source of all the love CHRIST bore. O my Redeemer! exclaims Simon de Cassia, at the foot of the Cross they part Thy garments, and on the Cross they divide Thy heart! Be thou present, O my soul, at this division of the heart, for, as the good JESUS yields His heart to be cut in sunder with the iron barb, it is a token that it will not be denied to thee.

S. Augustine observes as well, That there are many who part their garments and divide their effects among their kinsmen and friends; but only the SON of GOD bestowed in death His heart as a legacy—and not the heart only, but Himself with it.

S. Cyril remarks, That no sooner was CHRIST dead than His side was opened, and this in figure, that we might learn that when He died, the Gate of Glory was opened.

CHAPTER XXXIII.

Joseph of Arimathea.

"AFTER this, Joseph of Arimathea, being a disciple of JESUS, but secretly for fear of the Jews, besought Pilate that he might take away the body of JESUS: and Pilate gave him leave" (S. John xix. 38). S. Matthew says that he was a rich man; S. Mark that he was "an honourable counsellor, which also waited for the Kingdom of GOD," and that he "went in boldly unto Pilate, and craved the body of JESUS;" and S. Luke calls him "a counsellor, a good man, and a just;" and says that he "had not consented to the counsel and deed" of the chief priests and scribes.

The captain of the guard, or the centurion, having given notice that CHRIST was dead, Pilate yielded to the request of Joseph.

Before the SON of GOD ascended the Cross, and after He was on the Cross, and after He died upon the Cross, Joseph of Arimathea was the first to exhibit any sympathy and compassion by outward act. The thief and the centurion had addressed Him in words, but Joseph approached Him in acts. Let no man despair in troubles, let no man be dismayed in tribulation, for, when least expected, and where least looked for, some Joseph will be raised up by our Divine LORD to take us down from our cross, on which the world has racked us.

S. Jerome tells us, That it was most unusual for a criminal to be given private burial; and that licence to dispose of the body had always to be obtained from the magistrate who had condemned him.

Observe the great obedience of the SON of GOD. He would not be lifted up on the Cross without leave, and in obedience; and without leave, and in obedience, He would not descend from it. GOD, says S. Leo, doth highly esteem those who for love of Him obey others. We observe this in His SON, Who for obedience suffered on the Cross, and in obedience descended from it. His life lasted till He yielded up the ghost; but His obedience lasted till He was laid in the grave.

We must consider here who makes the request, what the request is, of whom it is made, how it is made, at what time it is made. He who makes the request is Joseph; the thing requested is the Body of JESUS; it is requested of the Roman Governor; it is made with great boldness, and on the same day that CHRIST suffered.

Details are often given us in Holy Scripture concerning persons eminent for some virtue or good work; thus, of Job it is said, "That man was perfect and upright, and one that feared GOD and eschewed evil." So of Joseph we are told that he was of Arimathea, that he was rich, a counsellor, a just man, and a secret disciple of JESUS.

First, he was called Joseph. Now this name is of good repute in Holy Scripture. To the first Joseph was committed the care of Israel in Egypt; to the second, the custody of the Incarnate WORD when a feeble Babe; to the third Joseph, the care of the Body of CHRIST after death. It seems as though the name Joseph belonged to those who were guardians of what was powerless to protect itself. Joseph sustained the famishing and feeble family of Jacob; Joseph protected the Holy Babe; Joseph took care of the soulless Body of CHRIST.

Joseph was of Arimathea, a village where the Priest Eli sat, where holy Hannah was born, where lived Elcanah her husband, where was neither idol nor idolatry. As Rama, we hear of it as the birth-place of Samuel the Prophet. It is remarkable that certain places seem to be blessed, and others appear to lie under a curse. Thus Sion, Bethlehem, and Rama were sacred, whilst Babylon, Jericho, Bethel, lay excommunicate.

Joseph was rich. Our LORD was buried by a rich man, to

teach us that the doing of works of mercy to the bodies of men appertains to the rich. Thus rich Tobias, like Joseph, was one who buried the dead. But Origen sees a further mystery in CHRIST making a grave with the rich in His death. He says that CHRIST died for rich as well as poor, and therefore He united the rich with the poor on Calvary; the rich to bury Him, the poor to weep over Him.

Joseph was a counsellor. We see that even in the most dangerous situations, in the worst society, the Saints of GOD may exist. The Council of the Jews slew CHRIST; but though Joseph was of the Council, he was not of their counsel. S. Augustine says: A man should be careful whom he trusts, and to whom he commits the care of his conscience, and seek out one of prudent counsel, and just as well, one of honour and rich in faith; for the SON of GOD committed Himself only to a man noble, rich, just, and a counsellor. Because He thus entrusted Himself to one devout and noble, He was taken down from the Cross, His wounds were anointed, His body was shrouded, and He was laid in a sepulchre. Evil men of bad counsel, if we join fellowship with them, will put us upon a cross, not take us down from one; strip us of all we have, rather than shroud us; bespatter us with dirt, and not anoint us; bury our fame and respect, certainly not regard and care for our bodies.

Joseph was a secret disciple of JESUS. CHRIST had three sorts of people surrounding Him; those who followed, but loved Him not; those who loved Him, but followed Him not; and those who both followed and loved Him. Of the first were the common people; of the second were Joseph and Nicodemus; of the last were S. John and the other Apostles. In our LORD there was no concealment. He preached openly, went openly, did His miracles openly. How is it, then, that He has concealed disciples? To this we answer, that, because it is natural to all to love life, there will always be some who serve CHRIST better in secret than openly. There were Martyrs who delivered themselves up to trial, and there were others who fled from martyrdom, but who, being caught, witnessed a good confession. These are not to be despised and regarded as no disciples, because they

Joseph of Arimathea.

have not the courage, the charity, or the faith of the others; their will, may not be so marked and perfect, yet, when occasion comes, those who seemed to be weakest often show the greatest courage and strength. Joseph was a disciple in secret, for fear of the Jews, before CHRIST was persecuted; but when persecution and death came, he showed fear of neither Jew nor Gentile, but "went in boldly" to Pilate to crave the Body of JESUS. In the reign of Jezebel and Ahab, when idolatry prevailed, there was one only professed and prominent believer, Elijah; but what said the LORD, "Yet I have left Me seven thousand in Israel, all the knees which have not bowed unto Baal, and every mouth which hath not kissed him" (1 Kings xix. 18).

Well observes Remigius: For the SON of GOD to entrust His precious Body to a secret disciple, and not to one who went openly with Him, is to teach us thereby that there are to this day many holy men and women in His Church who are secret and unknown to men, and yet are greatly esteemed of GOD, Who accepts them above others. He who had seen Judas and Joseph, the one an open disciple, the other a secret one; the one prominent and well known, the other scarce known to be a disciple, would have concluded that Judas was holy and Joseph was no Christian; but in the hour of need the open disciple betrays his Master, and the secret disciple buries Him. When the servants of the chief priests laid hands on CHRIST, the open disciples forsook Him and fled. When deserted of all, when, apparently, His promises had come to an end, His professions had come to nought, and His Kingship was ruined, then Joseph and Nicodemus, the timid and secret disciples, step forward, Joseph to lay the SAVIOUR in his own new tomb, and Nicodemus to embalm Him with spices.

Oh, what a comfort it is to all who will be good and serve GOD, to know that our LORD accepts the service of the secret disciple, as well as that of the open disciple; that is, that He takes and blesses the service, be it what it may, of wish or of work, done in company or alone, in sickness or in health, in adversity or in prosperity!

"Heaviness may endure for a night, but joy cometh in the morning" (Ps. xxx. 5). There is weeping and heaviness now as evening closes over Calvary; and little reck these mourners of the joy that will come on Easter morning.

At Prime CHRIST was accused; He received sentence at Tierce, He was crucified at Sext; at Nones, He died; and now, at Vespers, He is taken down from the Cross; whilst Compline will finish the day in the Grave.

Evening is come. Blessed Mary is at the foot of the Cross, surrounded by a few faithful ones, looking into the dead face of her CHRIST; and powerless to effect any thing. Must He hang there through the night? They have not ladders and pincers for removing Him; and even if they had, they have no licence from the Roman Governor to take Him down. They have no water to wash Him, no ointment wherewith to anoint Him, no shroud to wrap Him in, and no sepulchre in which to bury Him.

As the light dies out, greater grows the heaviness of the Virgin Mother. It is too late to hasten to the palace and ask for her SON'S Body. And how could she hope to obtain it, she being unknown to Pilate? She has no money to buy spices, she has no means to provide a winding-sheet, and she has no ground in which to bury Him.

Stupified in her woe, she stands and looks at her SON dragging on the nails, wan and relaxed in death. S. Mary Magdalene clasps the base of the Cross in tears. S. John endeavours to console the distressed Mother. Salome stays her up.

And up the hill, slowly, is coming Joseph with ladder and pincers, and Nicodemus bearing the shroud, the ointment, and the napkin.

Man's extremity is GOD'S opportunity. What the mourners had not dared to expect, that is about to happen.

The SON of GOD will be taken down from His Cross, will be washed, anointed, and laid in a seemly tomb.

CHAPTER XXXIV.

Joseph and Nicodemus.

"THE King of Ai he hanged on a tree until eventide: and as soon as the sun was down, Joshua commanded that they should take his carcass down from the tree" (Josh. viii. 29). Joshua was entering the Land of Promise at the head of the chosen people of GOD; but, before he could possess the land, he was compelled first to take the city Ai, and to hang the king of that city on a tree till evening, when his body was taken down and laid under a heap of stones.

What is signified by Joshua destroying Ai and hanging its king, reducing the city to a ruin, taking down the body of the king, burying it near the gate, building there an altar to the LORD, but the great work which was wrought on Calvary?

The Land of Promise is the Heavenly Country, the lot of our inheritance. Ai, that resisted Joshua, is the wicked Synagogue that withdrew her obedience from GOD, and fought against the great Captain of our Salvation. Ai was reduced by him to a heap of stones, and the Synagogue was left desolate, a ruin of hardened and obdurate sinners. The people of Israel could not enter the Promised Land till the King of Ai was hung on a tree; so, till CHRIST had crucified the old Adam, destroying the whole body of sin, having been made sin for us and nailing our rebellions, our iniquities, our transgressions in His own body to the tree—the Kingdom of Heaven was not opened to His elect.

Joshua having taken and despoiled Ai and made of it a ruinous heap, of the stones erected an altar to the LORD; so CHRIST, having destroyed the Synagogue, raised up of those stones children to faithful Abraham by the erection of His Church.

The King of Ai hung on the tree till the going down of the sun; and in like manner was CHRIST suspended on His Cross till the evening closed in. Hard by the gate was the King of Ai buried; and CHRIST was laid in the new tomb near the city which had brought upon itself sure destruction by fighting against GOD.

To return to Joseph. We see him, having obtained leave from Pilate to take CHRIST from His Cross, sharing his duties with Nicodemus, thereby teaching us not to be selfish in our enjoyment of religious privileges, but to seek out others and invite them to share these privileges with us, and especially those that be weak and of small courage, as was Nicodemus, who, for fear of the Jews, used to visit JESUS by night.

It is to be noted how these two, weak in courage, mutually strengthened each other. Those that be strong ought to bear the infirmities of the weak, and those whom Grace has strengthened may be able to lead on others, who, like themselves, are naturally of a fearful spirit and a timid nature. " It is not good for man to be alone," said GOD of the man He had made. And when CHRIST sent forth His disciples it was by two and two. So now these two come together to Calvary, each encouraging the other, each assisting the other.

Observe also that there is a time for all things; a time for profession of Faith, and a time for not forcing our convictions into public observation. Joseph and Nicodemus were long secret disciples, but, when the proper moment for the declaration of their Faith arrived, they unhesitatingly proclaimed it. And let it also be remarked that some profess their belief with their lips, and others by their acts. S. Peter said, "Thou art the CHRIST;" but in the garden he forsook his Master. Joseph and Nicodemus gave evidence of the firmness of their Faith, not by words but by deeds. And often greater are the deeds than the words. S. Peter's profession was made when CHRIST was alive and surrounded by disciples; that of the two old men was made when CHRIST was dead and deserted of the loudest professors.

These two honourable old men, having agreed together what

was to be done, sought ladders, pincers, a sheet for a shroud, ointments for embalming, knowing well that the Mother of CHRIST was too sad, too poor, too exhausted, to seek for these things.

Having divided their offices and charges, Joseph purchased the sheet, and Nicodemus bought the myrrh and aloes for the anointing of the sacred Body, with willing mind, and great bounty; for in Plato's words, When a man loves another, he does not reckon the expense of what he bestows on him he loves.

We do not read, says S. Leo, that any entreated Joseph and Nicodemus to crave of Pilate the Body of JESUS, nor yet to buy spices, nor to take CHRIST down from the Cross; but these aged men did this of their natural goodness, moved by charity. So let us not wait to be urged by others to undertake good and pious works, but let us ourselves look out for opportunities, and seeing them let us voluntarily embrace them.

"None shall appear before Me empty," saith GOD (Exod. xxiii. 15). That is, at the three principal feasts in the year, every Israelite shall go to the Temple of GOD, to render homage and to pray and offer sacrifice. And those who thus come to the Temple at the feasts shall not come with no offering, but shall bring with them something according as GOD has prospered them, as an oblation, in their hands.

Origen says, That he who is content with his "Our Father" and his Creed, and gives no alms, is one who appears empty before the LORD. It is well for him to say his prayers and to profess his Faith, but it is ill for him to offer nothing of his goods to his GOD. Better give a small alms than spend two hours in prayer.

S. Hilary observes, He goes empty before the LORD, who does a good work whilst obstinately persevering in sin; thus Cain sacrificed to GOD, but with hatred in his heart, therefore the LORD would not look on his offering. What doth it avail us, if we offer our goods to GOD and have not charity? What profit is there in our liberality to men, if we do not render to GOD that which is GOD'S.

Note and mark well, says Remigius, the law of GOD does not forbid thee to show thyself before Him, but only to present thyself before Him empty-handed.

Joseph and Nicodemus.

Joseph and Nicodemus observed the law of GOD when they prepared to appear before Him on His Cross. They would not go empty before their King; so, one carried myrrh and aloes, the other a shroud; so, like true and loyal disciples, they believed in Him with their hearts, they sought Him with their feet, they wept for Him with their eyes, they served Him with their wealth, and they anointed Him with their hands.

O my soul! buy a little myrrh and aloes, and accompany these venerable men to Calvary, for now, if ever, our LORD will suffer Himself to be touched and handled, embalmed and shrouded; and it may be, that, in recompense for this service, as thou layest Him in His grave, He will bury with Him all thine offences, and will raise thee from the death of sin. With the spices of thine affections, do thou anoint Him, O my soul, and with thy tears wash Him, and behold! as thou washest His sacred wounds, thine own sins will be cleansed.

Surely these aged disciples must have had trouble in procuring what was necessary, in getting a ladder here at a carpenter's, in procuring pincers there at a blacksmith's, at purchasing spices and linen in the market, in obtaining leave from Pilate, and in toiling up the hill of Calvary with the ladder on their shoulders. As the evening drew on, and the sun was going down, the Sabbath approached, when work must cease; therefore they had to make great speed to complete their undertaking.

O my soul! do thou accompany Joseph and Nicodemus along the well-trodden path by which, as on this morning, the rabble hurried to the sight. Thou wilt find it by the furrow made by the base of the Cross, as it was dragged along; by the red stains of Blood which dropped from the thorn-girt brow of CHRIST as He trod it; by the fragrance of the ointments borne by these honourable councillors. That pathway to Calvary is greatly privileged, it is trampled by the wicked, marked by the Cross of suffering, watered by the tears of penitence, perfumed with the spices of good works, and sanctified by the precious Blood of CHRIST.

CHAPTER XXXV.

The Descent from the Cross.

"I SAID, I will go up to the palm-tree, I will take hold of the boughs thereof" (Cant. vii. 8). That is, I will take a very high ladder, and I will ascend to the top of the palm-tree, and take hold of the branches, and pluck the fruit from off the tree.

In Divine and human learning the palm-tree is regarded as emblematical of Victory. Those who entered Rome in triumph had palm-leaf crowns; and all the martyr-host, as seen by S. John the Divine, had palm-boughs in their hands.

Origen, in commenting on this passage of the Song of Solomon, asks, What palm-tree has there ever been, or ever shall be in this world, like the Cross of CHRIST, on which He triumphed over the World and overcame the Devil? Oh, what a great difference there was betwixt the palm on which the SON of GOD triumphed and that which was used in triumph by the people of Rome. They, if we credit Livy, only conceded the palm to the soldier who had slain his enemy; but JESUS assumes the palm by being slain by His enemies.

O glorious Palm-tree, blessed Cross! on which JESUS first hung the Devil, crucified sin, atoned for the world, yielded up His own life, shed His own Blood, planted the Church, and opened the way to glory.

It certainly appears, O Good JESUS, that none ever triumphed, and none ever will triumph like Thee. Thou dost not bear the palm, but the palm Thee, to let us understand that the Cross did first triumph over Thy life, before Thou didst triumph over death.

There is but one tree and abundant fruit; and what is that fruit but the Flesh of CHRIST, whereof whosoever eateth shall live for ever. But now let us place our ladder against this tree, and let us, with Joseph and Nicodemus, go up into the palm-tree, and take hold of the boughs thereof, and gather the fruit.

Time was short, as the sun was near the horizon, and much had to be accomplished in a brief space. Joseph and Nicodemus consult with S. John and the Magdalen, and with their knees on the ground, and their grey heads uncovered, reverently kiss the Cross and worship Him Who is crucified thereon.

CHRIST was placed on the Cross by the hands of infidels; but it was by the hands of the faithful that He was removed from it.

Having done reverence to Him Who hung on the tree, they set their ladders against the Cross, and took the pincers in their hands; and, each with a hammer in his girdle, they mounted, step by step, one on either side.

Having reached the LORD, they beheld His face pale as ashes, His eyes dull and closed, His blood clotted, His hair draggled and knotted among the thorns, His bones out of joint, and His body covered with wounds and bruises. S. Cyprian exclaims, However much man may have written on the subject of the sufferings of CHRIST, it falls far short of what He endured.

Upon Jacob's ladder the Angels ascended and descended singing; but on that of Joseph are shed tears. There is joy and song in Heaven; on Calvary there is only heaviness and weeping.

The first thing that the two old men did, was to draw the cruel nails from the hands of CHRIST, and this they could not do without great difficulty, for the nails were of necessity large, and firm in the wood, and the dead sinews had contracted upon them. Thus they were constrained to smite with the hammer and work with the pincers; and each blow wrung the heart of the weeping Mother, who with wan face stood below, stayed up by Salome, and gazed on the awful scene.

S. Bernard says, I conjure you, Nicodemus, by the love you

bear Him Who hangs there, be gentle and spare your blows, for the Blessed Mother is ready to swoon beneath the Cross. Let not the drawing forth of the nails, which by entering slew the SON, slay now the Mother!

But, doubtless, with reverence and dexterity the earnest men wrought. And S. Anselm thinks that they gently struck, tenderly handled, easily withdrew, the nails from the pierced hands, and then washed them with their tears.

O glorious ladder, not of Jacob, by which Angels descend to men, but of CHRIST, by which men go up to GOD! My soul, do thou mount that ladder and contemplate thy LORD dead for thee; and do thou labour to undo that which crucified Him, and amend that which caused Him to die.

His hands having been detached from the arms of the Cross, the sacred Body of CHRIST leaned forward, and one of those above sustained it above, whilst another supported it below. Wondrous sight! These men held up the GOD Who at the same moment was sustaining their souls.

And now they draw out the long nail which was driven through the feet; and then they gently let down the dead Body of their GOD.

"It shall come to pass in that day, saith the LORD GOD, that I will cause the sun to go down at noon, and I will darken the earth in the clear day: and I will turn your feasts into mourning, and all your songs into lamentation; . . . and I will make it as the mourning of an only son, and the end thereof as a bitter day" (Amos viii. 9, 10). This, that was prophesied of old, has come to pass. The clear day was darkened; and the sun withdrew his light at noon; and there on Calvary was the mourning of the Only SON. Thenceforth the Jewish feasts were turned to mourning, and all their songs into lamentation, for their house was left unto the Jews desolate, and the curse was upon them and upon their children.

And now, indeed, as the red sun touches the western horizon, is the end of a bitter day; a day bitter in its beginning, bitter in its continuance, and bitter in its close; bitter in the hall of the Chief Priest, and bitter in the court of Pilate; bitter on the Way of Sorrows, bitter on Calvary; bitter on the Cross, and bitter to the Mother in its close, as the Body of her SON is laid on her lap, to be washed with her tears, anointed with the "mixture of myrrh and aloes, about a hundred pound weight," brought by Nicodemus (S. John xix. 39), and wrapped in the linen shroud.

CHAPTER XXXVI.

The Type of Jacob.

"AND there came also Nicodemus, which at the first came to JESUS by night, and brought a mixture of myrrh and aloes, about a hundred pound weight. Then took they the Body of JESUS, and wound it in linen clothes with the spices, as the manner of the Jews is to bury" (S. John xix. 39, 40). In like manner, when the Patriarch Jacob was dead in Egypt, his son Joseph "commanded his servants the physicians to embalm his father: and the physicians embalmed Israel" (Gen. l. 2). Having thus cared for the body of Jacob, Joseph went with it from Egypt, and conveyed it to Palestine, where he buried it in the cave of Machpelah.

S. Chrysostom observes that, as the works of the SON of GOD were many and great, so were the types that went before Him many in number and great in quality. And S. Augustine says that, as the thing prefigured exceeds the figure, and the substance excels the shadow it casts, so, without all comparison, the works done by CHRIST surpassed the types which foretold them.

Indeed, as the kernel surpasses in quality the shell, and the wheat excels the chaff, and the gold is more estimable than the crude ore, so much does CHRIST surpass all the figures which spoke of Him. All that the Patriarchs did may be imitated, all that the Prophets wrote may be understood; but the great miracles that were wrought by the SON of MAN none can imitate, and the depth of His teaching none can wholly fathom.

When Isaac bore the wood of the sacrifice on his shoulders

to the mountain, he was a type of CHRIST, Who should bear the Cross on His back up Calvary, on which to offer sacrifice for the sins of the world. But oh! how far greater was the antitype than the type! Isaac returned to his house alive, but JESUS hung on the wood of His Cross dead.

The serpent of brass which was erected in the wilderness was a figure of CHRIST on Mount Calvary, but the figure here again fell far short of that which it prefigured; for the serpent of brass healed only the bodies of those stung, whilst CHRIST on His Cross recovers men of the wounds of their souls.

When Moses brought Israel out of Egypt, again there was an earnest of the future mighty deliverance wrought by CHRIST. But that to which it pointed was the greatest deliverance of all. Moses brought the people from Egypt into the desert, but CHRIST leads His elect into Heaven.

Joseph between the butler and baker of Pharaoh, was a foreshadowing of CHRIST between the two thieves; but Joseph only promised the butler restoration to the servitude of his master's table, whilst JESUS promised the penitent thief the liberty of Paradise. The butler was to be raised after three days; but "To-day shalt thou be with Me in Paradise" was the promise of CHRIST.

Truly, from these few examples may be seen how the antitype surpasses the type, as the rose excels the thorn, as the fruit surpasses the leaf, as the truth is better than the dream, and the spirit than the letter.

When our Blessed LORD said, "Search the Scriptures; for in them ye think ye have eternal life; and they are they which testify of Me" (S. John v. 39), He plainly taught us to read the Sacred Writings with great diligence, else we should not understand the mysteries contained in them. To search is not to read carelessly and without attention; and unless we read with devotion and thought, we shall fail to detect their testimony to CHRIST. To search out a testimony as CHRIST commands us, requires care in seeking, time for finding, light whereby to discern, understanding with which to grasp, wisdom by which to retain, and love by which to enjoy that testimony which has been sought, found, discerned, grasped, and retained.

The Type of Jacob.

Coming then to our purpose, we note one of the types of the SON of GOD in Jacob the Patriarch, among the Fathers one of the most honourable and renowned, so that the Angel, in addressing the holy Virgin, says that her SON shall reign in the house of Jacob, singling Him out in preference to either Abraham or Isaac. Let us now search into the type of Jacob.

Jacob was at variance with his brother Esau on account of their father's inheritance, and so was CHRIST with the Jew touching the pre-eminence of His Church; but as, in the end, Jacob purchased the birth-right and inheritance of Esau for a mess of pottage, so CHRIST bought from the Synagogue its right and inheritance with His Blood. Jacob served for Leah and for Rachel his two wives; and CHRIST had first the Synagogue and then the Church. The Synagogue, weak-eyed like Leah, could not discern what was for its good, and was hated; whilst the Church, like Rachel, for whom the greatest toil was undergone, was the best loved.

Jacob died blind, his arms crossed, laden with years, surrounded by his children; and CHRIST gave up the Ghost on Calvary with His eyes dulled by tears, His arms stretched out on the Cross, weighed down with our offences, and with Jew and Gentile around.

At the point of death, and with the sign of the Cross, Jacob took away the heritage from his nephew Ephraim, the elder, to confer it on Manasses, the younger; and in like manner, at the last hour of life, and on the Cross, CHRIST disinherited the Synagogue, and gave the right of inheritance to the Church.

Jacob entered Egypt rich in gold, silver, and cattle, but when taken out of it, there were but the ointments and balm about his body. So CHRIST, the King of Glory, possessing all things, left this world in death, divested of all, exceeding poor, embalmed with the myrrh and aloes purchased by other men's money, and shrouded in a borrowed sheet.

Seeing, then, we have come from the figure to the thing figured, from the type to the antitype, from the shadow to the substance, it is expedient for us to say something about the ointments wherewith the SON of GOD was anointed, and the shroud in which He was wrapped.

CHAPTER XXXVII.

The Anointing of Christ.

THE SON'S Body having been placed in the Virgin-Mother's lap, and night approaching, dusk falling, and time being short, Joseph and Nicodemus were moved with great pity, and yet were constrained to ask the Mother to surrender to them the Body of her dear SON. The two honourable old men on one side beheld the SON resting on the lap on which, as an Infant, He had so often reposed, and were fain to let that wearied frame lie there where Nature pointed out its true place of sleep; but on the other side the approach of night constrained them to conquer their compassion, and proceed with their work.

"The LORD spake unto Moses, saying, Take thou also unto thee principal spices, of pure myrrh five hundred shekels, and of sweet cinnamon half so much, . . . and of sweet calamus two hundred and fifty shekels, and of cassia five hundred shekels, after the shekel of the sanctuary, and of oil olive an hin: and thou shalt make it an oil of holy ointment, an ointment compound after the art of the apothecary: it shall be an holy anointing oil" (Exod. xxx. 22—25).

In the ancient law, the tabernacle and all the vessels of the ministry, and the congregation, were anointed with this ointment. Without all doubt, this is a wonderful figure; but yet its accomplishment is more wonderful, for now on Calvary the Tabernacle of GOD among men, our EMMANUEL is anointed by the aged Joseph and Nicodemus, as was the old tabernacle by Moses and Aaron; and that ointment which embalmed the Tabernacle of CHRIST'S Body, now fills the whole house of His Church, and descends to every member of His congregation, as the oil on Aaron's beard ran down to the skirts of his clothing.

Tell me, I pray you, when GOD commanded in the Law of Moses that odoriferous perfumes should be offered in His sanctuary, did He care for the fragrance, like a man, or had this law a spiritual significance? Most certainly, when the HOLY GHOST inspired these laws, deeper mysteries were taught than the blind Jew discerned on the surface.

Let it be noted that there were many conditions to be fulfilled in the anointing with the holy oil. GOD commanded it to be made of only sweet and odoriferous spices; also these spices were very costly and precious; they were to be such as the law named, and not indiscriminately selected scented gums. None were to be wanting, and none were to be added thereto. They were to be accurately measured, and that, not by the secular and common scale, but weighed by the sacred shekel of the sanctuary. What is the holy Tabernacle but the Body of CHRIST? This is the Hill to which we lift up our eyes, this the Tower to which we betake ourselves for safety, this our City of refuge, this the Tabernacle in which we will dwell, and this, too, the Temple in which we must worship.

What were the aromatic spices which were offered by the Priest?—but the most holy virtues of the SON of GOD, whose fragrance fills the world, and of which the congregation of the elect are made to partake. On Calvary, where had been the odour of decaying carcasses, was now the fragrance of sweet spices. There, where all our sins and iniquities were offensive in the nostrils of GOD, is now the sweet-smelling savour of the perfected humility, obedience, love, long-suffering, and patience of CHRIST. As the wood cast by Moses into the bitter waters sweetened them, so the fetor of Calvary is made aromatic by the virtues of CHRIST.

What other things are those four sweet perfumes with which GOD commanded the holy Sanctuary to be made sweet;—but the bitter myrrh of suffering, the sweet cinnamon of charity, the calamus of patience, and the cassia of obedience?

All the odours were of exact measure by careful weighing, to let us understand that the SON of GOD did equally and indifferently shed His Blood for all, great or small, rich or poor, living or dead. Origen says, Often our LORD bestows His favours more or less, when He pleases, and how He pleases, and to whom He pleases, yet to all is sufficient by measure. S. Anselm, in an Epistle, writes, What do I care, my Brother, that thou art stronger than I, more noble in blood, more beautiful in body, more renowned in dignity, seeing that we are created by One GOD, and redeemed by One CHRIST, and governed by One HOLY GHOST? What does it mean, that of cinnamon there should be two hundred and fifty shekels, and of calamus the same amount? —but that CHRIST shed His Blood as much for the labouring man who cuts stubble as for the prince who sits upon a throne. And what does it mean, that of myrrh there should be five hundred shekels, and an equal amount of cassia?—but that, however great might be the sufferings of CHRIST, His obedience was equal in measure thereto.

S. Chrysostom says, When the SON of GOD imparted His precious Blood, He gave in excess to none, nor gave too little to any, nor deprived any wholly of it; but afterwards it had greater force in some than in others, but the fault lies with those to whom it is entrusted, not with Him Who entrusts it. What is the meaning of this, that all these sweet spices were pounded in a mortar before they were offered in the temple, and, having been ground very small, were carefully sifted, and then mixed into a mass with oil? Surely it points to the bruising and crushing of our Blessed LORD in His great sufferings on this day of trial and rebuke, and to the mingling with all the virtues He exhibited, and wherewith His congregation were to be anointed, His most precious Blood. And with respect to us, if our virtues and works are to be accepted of GOD, they must be crushed in sincere contrition, and sifted by self-examination, and fused in the oil of Divine Unction.

Unground is the spice man offers to GOD, who thinks on the Passion of CHRIST with no broken and sorrowful spirit; and unsifted are the aromatic gums and woods man presents, when he reads or listens to the account of the Sufferings of CHRIST without meditating upon them; and unmingled are the fragrant particles with oil, when he reads and meditates on the Death of

CHRIST as a mental exercise, without the HOLY SPIRIT to melt them into an ointment wherewith to anoint all his acts and all his thoughts.

The spices were to be weighed with the shekel of the Sanctuary. "All thy estimations shall be according to the shekel of the Sanctuary" (Lev. xxvii. 25). The Jews had two sorts of measures and weights, those used for profane purposes, and those employed in sacred things. The profane weight was the stater, whilst that used in weighing all things connected with the Temple was the shekel. Thus every thing which was in common use, which went into the market, was estimated by the stater, whilst every sacred estimation was "according to the shekel of the Sanctuary."

S. Augustine says, In thee and in me, all we do, all we think, is only of the common weight, sometimes good, sometimes bad: the perfumes of our prayers are sometimes weighed with devotion, sometimes with coldness; but far otherwise was it with the love and zeal of the SON of GOD. Time increased them not, nor trouble made them cold. With the weight of the Sanctuary were the works of CHRIST weighed, whilst ours are tried by a different measure. His works could not be weighed with the same weight as are ours. The merits of one Holy Man may be measured with the merits of another Saint; and the constancy and torments of one Martyr may be compared with the constancy and the torments of another; but the virtues, and the sufferings, and the endurance of CHRIST must be weighed with another balance, and must not be put into the scale with the works of men. The HEIR of Eternity doth not enter into our account, nor is He tried by our measure. He is not weighed where we are weighed, nor judged as we are judged. How is it possible to weigh Him Who weighs all things? How is it possible to measure Him Who measures all things by His wisdom?

Above, in the resting-place of the TRINITY, and in the depth of the Divinity, the SON of the Living GOD has His measure and weight; but the measure and weight of the Sanctuary are not as the measure and weight of our world below. No pains of Martyrs can be compared with the pains of CHRIST, no holiness of Angels can be meted against His, no majesty of monarchs can enter the scale with the splendour of the KING of Kings.

In the balance of the Sanctuary nothing was weighed but that which was of the Sanctuary; and so in the balance of CHRIST, His works alone are weighed. As we could not weigh ourselves in His balance, He came to us, and erecting that balance on Calvary, on the arms of the Cross He weighed our offences against His virtues, our rebellion against His obedience, our guilt against His Blood, and satisfied for all with His overabounding merits.

CHAPTER XXXVIII.

The Right maintained.

AND now, whilst the two aged counsellors, S. John, the Blessed Virgin, and the rest are proceeding from Calvary to the grave, let us consider the words of David : " Thou hast maintained My right and My cause : Thou art set in the throne that judgest right " (Ps. ix. 4).

Many great mysteries are contained in the Psalm from which this passage is quoted, and it behoves us, in meditating on them, to set before our eyes first, Who is He Who maintains the cause, and sits in the throne? then, What is the place where the right is maintained, and whence judgment is given? and lastly, Whose cause is taken in hand by Him?

He Who maintains the cause is CHRIST; the place where it was maintained was the Cross ; and he whose cause was maintained was Man. What prince wrought such great things fighting as did JESUS on His throne? Who ever obtained such a great victory by hard battle as did He by enduring the contradiction of sinners? What judge ever maintained a cause on his seat, as did CHRIST on the throne of His Cross? O glorious Throne! on which He was accompanied by thieves, crowned with thorns, robbed of His Blood, deprived of His friends, encompassed by enemies !

To this throne CHRIST was sentenced by Pilate the governor. How then is it said that thence He deals judgment? On this throne He is robbed of His honour and right; how then can He on it maintain my cause?

Sitting on the throne of the Cross, the SON of GOD judged him who judged, that is the World ; judged that which was deserving of judgment, that is Sin; judged that which had sentenced Him, that is Injustice. Oh, how well the Prophet says, "Thou hast maintained my right and my cause," when it was my right and my cause which necessitated Thy crucifixion. By Thy death on the Cross Thou didst obtain for me a right to enter Heaven, by Thy pleading Thou didst maintain my cause against my great adversary, the Devil. Thou art my Advocate, Thou art my Judge, Thou art my Deliverer.

On Mount Calvary JESUS was crucified and died, not for His own cause, but for mine; not because He was guilty, but because I was the transgressor. Then He maintained my cause, when by the surrender of Himself to death He saved me from death eternal. Then He maintained my right, when He suffered for my wrong and made over to me His right. Then He judged on His throne, when He divested Satan of his power and took me from the hands of the destroyer.

"Thou hast maintained my right and my cause" when of one ignorant Thou didst make me wise, when from a slave Thou didst make me a son, when from an alien Thou didst change me into a fellow-citizen, when from condemnation Thou didst set me free. Then didst Thou take my cause in hand, when to the prejudice of Thy Person Thou didst seek only the saving of my soul. I repeat, to the prejudice of Thy Person, for Thou didst suffer Thy Body to be mangled, bereft of life, and transfixed with a spear in death, only in order that my cause might be finished.

"Thou hast maintained my right and my cause." When Thou didst come down from the glory of Heaven, and lay aside Thy splendour, it was for my sake, for my cause. When of One invisible Thou didst make Thyself visible, when of One impassible Thou didst become passible, when of One immortal Thou didst become mortal; when from being LORD of Angels Thou didst become an outcast of men, then Thou didst take my right and my cause in hand.

Oh, how Thou didst plead my cause, seeing that, in order to elevate me, Thou didst abase Thyself; in order to give me honour, Thou didst divest Thyself of dignity and embrace infamy; in order to deliver me, Thou didst suffer Thyself to be taken; in order to excuse me, Thou didst permit men to condemn Thee!

"Thou hast maintained my right and my cause" on the Cross, where, like an advocate, Thou didst pray for me; where, like a judge, Thou didst pardon me; where, like a kinsman, Thou didst pay for me; where, like a brother, Thou didst answer for me; where, like a friend, Thou didst die for me; where, like a father, Thou didst weep for me.

"Thou hast maintained my right and my cause" on Thy Royal Throne of the Cross, where Thou didst hear me and the Devil, and the Devil and me, as we stood before Thee seated in judgment; then he claimed me as his slave, then he accused me of sin; and lo! Thou didst refuse me to him, by claiming me as Thine own, and didst discharge the accusation by suffering Thyself the penalty. And as the Eternal FATHER was wroth with me because I have broken His commandments, and have not walked in His statutes, nor loved His law, Thou didst maintain my cause before Him, pleading Thy sufferings, offering Thy Blood, expiating with Thy death.

"Thou hast maintained my right and my cause" with the Angels, in giving them charge to guard me. "Thou hast maintained my right and my cause" with the Church, by incorporating me in her. "Thou hast maintained my right and my cause" with Satan, by delivering me out of his hands. "Thou hast maintained my right and my cause" against Sin, by pardoning it.

"Thou hast maintained my right and my cause," not having need or reason to do it, seeing Thou didst create me in Thy image, redeem me with Thy Blood, endow me with Thy merits, heal me with Thy wounds, enlighten me with Thy doctrine, draw me to Thine elect, and reform me with Thy Sacraments; not that I deserved all this, but that Thou of Thy wondrous and overflowing love didst will it. O Light of my eyes and Rest of my soul! upon my knees I beseech Thee, and with tears I ask Thee, that Thou wouldest lighten my understanding, cleanse my heart, guide my thoughts, that I may worthily meditate on all the great mysteries of Thy Passion, on all the awful and solemn events of that scene where Thou didst maintain my right and my cause.

And now the work is over, CHRIST on His entry into the

world undertook my cause, He has now pleaded it, and has maintained it unto the end. The work is finished, the Advocate has won, but His victory has cost Him His life. He has maintained my right and my cause without a thought of laying it down. Though the Jews bid Him come down from the Cross and make an end of His sufferings, He would not desert that throne, for thereon must He sit to judge my cause, and thereon must He remain till it was brought to an end.

But now all is over, and now that my cause is won, and my right is made clear, He leaves His throne in weariness for His bed in the cool and quiet grave.

CHAPTER XXXIX.

The Entombment.

"HE came again, and said, Father, one of our nation is strangled, and is cast out in the market-place. Then, before I had tasted of any meat, I started up, and took him up into a room until the going down of the sun. .... And after the going down of the sun I went and made a grave, and buried him" (Tob. ii. 3, 4. 7). These are the words of Holy Scripture, speaking of the care which the good man had to bury the dead. For there was in Babylon a poor man executed by injustice, which, when it was known to Tobit, he brought him secretly into his house, and at sunset he buried him in a new grave. Among the Works of Mercy, the burying of the dead is very acceptable to GOD, as is also the visiting of the sick, the which two works always receive a reward of our LORD.

When Saul was slain upon the mountains of Gilboa, King David sent great thanks to the inhabitants of Jabesh-gilead because they had reverently buried the body of the King. "Blessed be ye of the LORD, that ye have showed this kindness unto your lord, even unto Saul, and have buried him. And now the LORD show kindness and truth unto you: and I also will requite you this kindness, because ye have done this thing" (2 Sam. ii. 5, 6).

Holy Scripture also highly commends Jehu for burying the body of Jezebel because she had been a king's daughter, after that, for her iniquity, she had been slain. And also Joseph is had in honour because he brought the bones of his father out of Egypt to be buried in Palestine. The great Simon commanded a stately monument to be erected in Modin, in which he buried his brothers, the Maccabees, and reserved a place for his own bones.

But to come to our purpose. The SON of GOD, Holy JESUS, did not build Himself a sepulchre when He was alive, nor did His Mother know where to lay Him when He was dead; and, as He had not where to lay His head in life, He had not where to lay His head in death. Alive, He lived in friends' houses; and dead, He reposed in another man's tomb.

How should He make Himself a tomb, when He had not a house to dwell in? On the Altar of the Cross He remembered well to pray for His enemies, to pardon the thief his sins, but He gave no thought to where He was to be buried, for He sought not Himself, but us.

"Now in the place where He was crucified there was a garden; and in the garden a new sepulchre, wherein was never man yet laid. There laid they JESUS therefore" (S. John xix. 41, 42). Hard by unto the Mount Calvary was a little garden on the hill-slope, in which, in the face of the rock, was a tomb, newly hewn, in which none had yet been laid; and there CHRIST was placed.

If we examine the words of the holy Evangelist, we see that there are several remarkable particulars recorded of this grave. It was in the rock, unused, and it belonged to another man. All which conditions were necessary. For if the tomb had not been of stone, the Jews might have had some colour for their lie, when they asserted that the disciples had stolen the Body away. If it had not been new, they might have supposed the Resurrection to have been that of some other than CHRIST. If it had not been the property of another, and he a counsellor of the Sanhedrim, they might have believed that the Resurrection was feigned.

O Poor LORD! did it not content Thee to be born without a house, and to live without wealth, and to die without a bed; but must Thou lie in another man's grave? Oh, how happy should I be, if Thou wouldst bury Thyself in this soul of mine, that, as Thou didst rise the third day, never after to die again, so I might, with Thee, be raised to newness of life.

The grave had no inscription over it, the door was open, the stone was on one side; and now the attendants with loving hands lift the Body of CHRIST, spread the sheet on the floor of the tomb, and lay the sacred Corpse on it, and then gently wrap and veil it, ere they close the sepulchre and retire.

There, then, remained JESUS in the cave, covered with the stone, alone, anointed with rich ointments, His winding-sheet wet with the tears of those who had entombed Him.

O Love of my soul, Light of my eyes, Joy of my heart, Rest of my life, tell me, I pray Thee, how, being the LORD of Life, canst Thou lie dead and shrouded in a poor grave?

Why, O Good JESUS, didst Thou not elect some sumptuous tomb? Why didst Thou not summon the choirs of Heaven to chant Thy requiem, and the hosts of Angels to lay Thee to rest?

O Good JESUS, how much more am I bound unto Thee for redeeming me, than for creating me; for in making me, Thou didst only give me myself; but in redeeming me, Thou didst give me Thyself. Thou didst give me Thyself when I was a stranger from Thee through sin, reconciling me by grace, making me Thy brother by nature, and Thy companion in glory.

Oh, how much more do I owe Thee for having re-made me, than for having first created me! For when I was first made, Thou didst give me nothing; but when Thou didst redeem me, Thou didst bestow on me all Thy wealth. In creating the world Thou wast occupied six days, and in redeeming me Thou wast engaged thirty and three years; in Thy speech receiving contradiction, in Thy doing walking amidst snares, in Thy torments an object of mockery, in Thy miracles surrounded by blasphemers.

CHAPTER XL.

Conclusion.

O GLORY of Jerusalem, Joy of Israel, at the instant Thou didst assume human flesh, then began the travail of Thy soul and the sufferings of Thy body. What was CHRIST'S most holy life, but a long and cruel Passion? What did Holy JESUS not suffer? what did He not endure? seeing that in every age He was troubled, by all people He was persecuted, in all parts of His body He was tormented! He suffered in His eyes, shedding tears; in His ears, hearing blasphemies; in His face, feeling buffets; in His mouth, tasting gall and vinegar; in His hands and feet, enduring wounds; in His head, thorns; in His heart, a spear-point. In the manger He endured poverty; in the desert, persecution; in Egypt, exile; in the temple, resistance; in the way, weariness; in the garden, sweat; and on the Cross, death. In the day-time He taught; in the night-time He prayed. From the hour of His birth till the moment of His entombment, what time was there in which He did not some good? And for whom, and to whom, was that good done, but Man?

At the Hour of Lauds JESUS is seized, at Prime He is accused, at Tierce scourged at the pillars, at Sext condemned, at Nones put to death, at Vespers anointed, at Compline buried. Oh, how at each hour He does and suffers for man! He, the Judge, for man is judged; He, the King, for man is mocked; He, the Priest, for man is, as the victim, slain; He, the Innocent, for guilty man suffers. Oh, wondrous mystery! He suffered in friend and in foe; and friend and foe helped Him to suffer. He suffered

Conclusion. 171

in the weeping women, and in the accusing infidels; in the blaspheming and in the penitent thief; in the soldier who pierced Him, and in the Mother, pierced through with many sorrows.

Infinite was the love of my LORD and my GOD, for nothing could induce Him to leave His Cross till He had wrought out my salvation—no, not the hardness of the bed, nor the bitter drink, nor the grievous torment, nor the cruel death, nor the love of His Mother, nor the shame of nakedness, nor the persuasion of the people, nor the ingratitude of the world.

O Good JESUS, Love of my soul! what charity is this that overcomes Thee? What love is this that guides Thee, that, when asked to descend from the Cross, Thou dost refuse, and yet that makes Thee mount Thy Cross unasked? What am I, that Thou shouldst suffer thus for me, when I am conceived in sin, born in pain, brought up in ignorance, powerless to resist evil, ready to yield to sin, inconstant in virtue? May my soul mark with attention, and consider with gravity, Who this is Who has suffered for me, where He has suffered, how He has suffered, and for whom He has suffered; all which, if rightly considered, will fill me with amazement, and humility, and shame.

What can I present unto thee, O LORD, in return for all Thou hast done for me? What can I give Thee, but the Blood Thou didst shed for me? What can I offer Thee, but only the charity Thou didst bear for me? All this I offer Thee on my knees, presenting it to Thee with many tears, hoping that it may profit me.

Finally, I present unto Thee, O my Good JESUS, all this work and the author of the same, to the end that it may profit Thy servants, and that the glory may redound unto Thee, and to no other; and, if it be not perfect, then, O Good JESUS, I pray Thee to supply that which may be wanting.

Trino et Uni sit Laus.

GILBERT AND RIVINGTON,
PRINTERS,
ST. JOHN'S SQUARE, LONDON.

www.ingramcontent.com/pod-product-compliance
Lightning Source LLC
Chambersburg PA
CBHW020243170426
43202CB00008B/200